M is for
MUM

Maeve Bradbury is a freelance journalist and copywriter. She is the author of *How to be a Domestic Goddess* (Apple Press) and the popular blog The Happy Housewife. She has a degree from Oxford University in English Literature and a diploma in European Culture. Having worked as a professional cook in a previous existence, she now lives in domestic bliss with her husband and four sons.

M is for
MUM

Maeve Bradbury

APPLE

First published in the UK in 2009 by
Apple Press
7 Greenland Street
London
NW1 0ND
www.apple-press.com

Conceived and produced by
Elwin Street Limited
3rd Floor, 144 Liverpool Road
London N1 1LA
www.elwinstreet.com

ISBN 978-1-84543-317-8

Designed by Jon Wainwright, Alchemedia Design
Illustrated by Micca/Dutch Uncle
Cover image: The Art Archive

10 9 8 7 6 5 4 3 2 1

Printed in Singapore

Contents

Introduction

Becoming a mother is like starting out on a big adventure. You're not really sure what kit you might need and whether you have been on the right training course. Unfortunately children don't come with a manual or a set of operating instructions – a major fault in the manufacturing process, if you ask me. As with any voyage into the unknown, it would be awfully helpful to have a map. However, motherhood is one of those journeys that doesn't have a recognised route, you'll be travelling off-piste most of the way, so there really isn't much point asking 'are we nearly there yet?' (A question you will later become familiar with on long car journeys . . .)

So I can't provide you with a set of co-ordinates or prepare you for the all the many experiences, surprises and obstacles you may encounter, but I hope the advice in this book will offer a few signposts on your way. A mother can always do with an extra hand (especially when one is fully occupied with holding a baby), and some useful advice to help deal with all the demands upon her time.

Being a mum is likely to be the most difficult, challenging and, of course, rewarding job you've ever had. It is unpaid work too, and in my experience you're unlikely to get much gratitude from them until you're an old lady. You really need to be a jack of all trades. You have to perfect the art of kissing things better; be a dab hand at wielding double-sided sticky tape; know how to turn an ordinary sandcastle into a sea-shell encrusted fortress, appropriately defended by a moat; throw a children's birthday party that is the envy of every mother in your neighbourhood; and be able to put your mascara on at the traffic lights because there just wasn't time before you dashed out of the house. And you might occasionally be called upon to do it all at the same time!

I hope this book will give you some ideas to cover all the bases, from being a caring mum, looking after colds and fevers and baking the best cupcakes in town, to the practical considerations, like changing nappies, how to get the cleaning done quickly, and avoiding temper tantrums whenever possible. With picnics and party games, you can be an entertaining mum too, and obviously you'll need to know how to fashion a pirate costume and turn macaroni into priceless jewellery. You can even try your hand at some advanced skills, like creating your own little private corner to retreat to, tackling teenage romance, shaking up a martini, or making sure you get a night off now and then, with or without your husband.

No matter how much your life may be changed by motherhood, the rewards are immeasurable. That first smile when he recognises your face, the first faltering steps into your outstretched arms, the way he looks into your eyes with total trust . . . there is no job in the world that can come as close to making you feel like you've struck gold. When he eventually calls you 'Mum,' your heart will never quite recover.

Caring Mum

- ✢ Treating cuts and scrapes
- ✢ Soothing a crying baby
- ✢ Telling a bedtime story
- ✢ Helping with homework
- ✢ Making homemade ice cream

Caring for your kids is an important job for mums. Cuddling them comes naturally to most of us, but what do you do when they get the sniffles, are cutting their first teeth, need help with their homework or don't want to go to bed? This chapter gives you helpful advice on some of the common problems mums face. Basic first aid, recipes for healthy foods and sweet treats, and even helping them get through the first day at school, are just some of the things you'll discover to help you be a Caring Mum.

First aid

It is essential to have a well-stocked first aid kit in your home. Store it in a secure place where small children cannot get at it, but where everyone else in the house will have easy access. Remember to keep it fully stocked at all times – when you use something, replace it right away, and regularly check the use-by dates of medication; you never know when an emergency may occur. It is also a good idea to enclose some basic first aid principles – either handwritten or a first aid manual.

To include in your first aid kit:

- ❖ adhesive tape
- ❖ sterile gauze
- ❖ different sized bandages
- ❖ antibiotic ointment
- ❖ antiseptic solution
- ❖ painkillers

- ❖ hydrocortisone cream
- ❖ sharp scissors
- ❖ safety pins
- ❖ tweezers
- ❖ thermometer

Cuts and scrapes

Sometimes it's baffling how they happen. The fact is they do, and there's really very little you can do to avoid it. Cuts and scrapes are a fact of life when you have children, especially for older babies who are crawling, pulling up, and just learning to walk. All you can do is learn to pick up the pieces as best you can. If your baby gets a bump, here's what to do.

How to dress cuts and scrapes

> ⤳ If a cut or scrape is bleeding, apply direct pressure until the bleeding stops.
> ⤳ For cuts, wash the area with warm water and soap to remove any dirt. If dirt is present in the cut, try to get it out by running warm water over the cut to flush it out. Don't poke around in the cut to get dirt out, as this may cause more damage.
> ⤳ Scrapes need washing too. Use a washcloth or a cotton ball soaked with warm water, and gently dab the scrap or abrasion to remove any dirt.
> ⤳ Cover the cut or scrape with a plaster.
> ⤳ If the cut or scrape is minor, uncover the area at night to let the wound dry out and heal faster. Cover it again in the morning if need be. If you notice any signs of infection, such as redness, swelling and pus, take your baby to the doctor.

Soothe a crying baby

When small babies cry it means they really are trying to tell you they want something, and it's usually something quite simple, like food, sleep or a nappy change. This is the life of your small baby and this is the mental checklist you'll have down rote before the end of your first few hours looking after her. Your parents and every adult in your (now diminishing) social circle will likely give you advice on getting your baby to stop crying. And they will tell it to you in the most confident of manners. Of course, the answer is to do what works for your baby and you, but there are certain basic things to check for and some tried-and-true techniques to get you started.

Top ways to get your baby to stop crying

⬧ Check the nappy.
⬧ Try feeding her.
⬧ It might be that your youngster is tired and needs help getting to sleep.
⬧ Offer a pacifier or your washed little finger for her to suck on.
⬧ Swaddle a small baby so she'll feel secure and hold her against the warmth of your tummy.
⬧ Take a stroll with your baby in the carrier, or rock gently in a rocking chair.
⬧ Take her for a drive – the motion of the car can be soothing.
⬧ Sing softly or play music for her.

Teething

Teething is what happens when a baby's first teeth begin pushing through the gums. This usually happens around six months, though it can be as early as three months or as late as one year. In most cases, you'll be able to see the end of the tooth on the gum, starting with the bottom incisors first, then the top ones (the last molars will come in around age three). If you can't see a tooth, you can guess your baby is teething if she's drooling a lot, has a low fever or diarrhoea, and is eager to chew on things. As you can imagine, it's a painful time and many babies get irritable. You can't stop the teeth from coming in, so the best you can do is make her as comfortable as possible.

How to help a teething baby

* Teething babies like to chew on things – anything – because the pressure on the gums and new teeth coming in helps relieve the pain. Teething rings, teething biscuits, or even fingers will help.
* Cold things to chew on feel good for your baby and it helps to numb the pain a little. Try giving her a frozen banana, a clean, icy washcloth, a cold carrot stick, or chill a teething ring in the freezer.
* If your baby is eating solids, cold apple sauce and yoghurt are welcome foods.
* An infant dose of acetaminophen will help the pain and reduce fever if she has one. Check with your doctor before doing this.

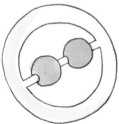

Colds and fevers

Having a sick baby can be a very stressful time for a parent, even if it's only a mild affliction. If your baby comes down with a cold or a fever, there are some things you can try to alleviate her symptoms. The best way to prevent a cold is to keep your and any older kids' hands washed, and to ask anyone to wash their hands before holding your baby. Also, keep her away from people who do have colds – they'll understand.

What to do if your baby has a cold

- ✧ Give older babies lots of fluids and vitamin C. Babies who are breastfeeding have all the fluids they need. They're also less likely to get a cold because they have their mum's immunities during that time.
- ✧ Put on a vaporizer while your baby is sleeping to help open up nasal passageways.
- ✧ Elevate your baby's head while she is sleeping by propping the mattress up with a rolled-up towel.
- ✧ Babies less than one year old should only be given cold medicine like decongestants if you've checked with the doctor first.
- ✧ Water is the best decongestant available.
- ✧ Give older babies pineapple. The enzymes in it help break down thick mucus and help with decongestion.

A feverish baby

Lots of things can give a small baby a fever: teething, a cold, allergies, new immunisations, or too many blankets, to name a few. And most of the time, a fever is a good thing; it's how the body fends off invading bacteria and viruses. As a general rule, babies tend to have higher fevers than adults do, so unless the temperature is over 37.8°C (100°F), then there's really no reason for concern, especially if she is eating normally. Instead, take note of your baby's behaviour. If she is lethargic, has stopped eating, or is crying a lot, then you should call your doctor. In the meantime, calmly try a few of the following steps.

What to do if your baby has a fever

- If your baby is bundled up, try removing the blankets and sweaters. That will often drop the temperature at least a little.
- Give the appropriate dose of infant's acetaminophen (brand name: Tylenol) or ibuprofen. For the youngest babies, check with your doctor first to make sure this is okay.
- Get a cloth wet with warm water, wring it out, and gently smooth the damp cloth over your baby's forehead, neck, and body, letting the water air-dry on her skin. Take care not to use cold water and definitely do not put her in a tub of cold water. That can actually have the reverse effect and raise the temperature, as the body has to work harder to overcome the shock of having cold water put on it.
- Turn down heaters and turn on a fan.
- Keep your baby hydrated either with breast milk or, if she's eating solids, water or a water-electrolyte solution.

Checking temperatures

You will probably already have an idea that your baby has a fever simply by touching her forehead with your lips — a time-tested method for temperature-taking by mums and dads the world over. Taking her temperature with a thermometer can reinforce what you already know but it can also be a way to see if medicine or other treatments are working.

Having a good thermometer around the house is essential, and there are several different kinds; the underarm thermometer and the ear thermometer are the most common. Oral thermometers just don't work with infants or even toddlers, because it's impossible to get even the slimmest amount of co-operation from your crying, squirming young one. In fact, dealing with your baby's protests can be the hardest part of taking a temperature. Any time you take a baby's temperature, no matter what the method, make sure she is as calm as you can possibly make her. Intense crying can raise the body temperature and give you a distorted reading. Don't persist beyond reasonable attempts. If your baby is very uncomfortable and struggling actively and mightily, then remove the thermometer and try a different method a little later on.

Underarm or auxillary thermometer

The most common thermometer and the easiest to use — especially for squirmy babies — is the kind that you put under a baby's armpit. Most baby supply stores sell these with digital readouts that are run on small camera batteries. They're reliable, cheap, and, as they turn off automatically, you shouldn't ever have to change the battery. Oral thermometers or rectal ones will also work if placed snugly in a baby's armpit; it takes about five minutes to get a reading. Temperatures taken under the arm are a full degree lower than what is normal orally, so always add a degree to an underarm temperature.

Ear or tympanic thermometer

If you do get one of these, ask the doctor to show you how to use it properly. Some doctors warn that it can be difficult to place this thermometer in the ear canal exactly right, especially with small babies younger than three months. In some cases doctors will even ask you to double-check the temperature using a different method. In theory, what you do is put the end of the thermometer in your baby's ear, press a button and in seconds you have an accurate temperature. The idea is that there's very little struggling to get the job done and it offers the least discomfort for your baby.

Taking a baby's temperature (underarm)

1 Remove her shirt and sit her in your lap. Make sure her underarm is dry.
2 Lift up her arm and place the end of the thermometer in her armpit so that the thermometer rests in the fold of her arm.
3 Lower her arm over the thermometer and hold her elbow against her side with one hand. Make sure the thermometer is snug under the arm and not sticking out the other side.
4 Digital underarm thermometers blink off and on until an accurate temperature has been taken. This can take three to five minutes.

Baby massage

Massaging your young one is a great way for the two of you to bond. It's relaxing, it stimulates your baby's muscles, and some say gently massaging the stomach can help ease gas pains in the stomach. Massaging your baby may even help improve sleep patterns and strengthen her tiny immune system. Regardless, it's a good fun, physical thing you and your baby can do to spend time together.

1 Touching mainly with the palms of both hands, gently spread your hands over your baby's head. Repeat three times.
2 Use the palms of your hands to rub your baby's chest by placing your hands together in a prayer manner. With hands together and your thumbs closest to you, gently touch the centre of the chest with your little fingers. Now slowly open your hands outward over the chest so that your fingers and palms touch her soothingly. Repeat on your baby's back.
3 Massage your baby's arms by 'milking' them. Very gently grip her arm with one hand and pull it towards her wrist as if you were milking a cow. When one hand gets to the wrist, start with the other hand just under the shoulder and so on. Repeat on her legs.
4 Next, roll your baby's arms gently between your hands. Place the arm on one palm and sandwich it with the other hand. Rapidly 'roll' the arm back and forth in a quick, short manner. Repeat on your baby's legs.

Take great care when giving
your baby a massage. It is not
like adult massage, you have to be
very gentle – much gentler than
you might think. Try closing your
eyes and pressing gently on your
eyelids without causing any
discomfort – that is about the
amount of pressure you should use.

Nap times

Getting your young one down for a nap can be a tricky task, especially because you don't want to botch the job and end up with a tired and crying baby – a combination that complicates the task tenfold. Bear in mind that research done by the American Academy of Pediatrics now shows that it is safer to put babies to sleep on their backs rather than their stomachs. However, some researchers say that you should put them on their side, especially if they tend to spit up a lot. Put a rolled up blanket behind them so they can't roll onto their back, but don't put them so far on their side that they'll roll over onto their stomach.

It's also not a good idea to let your baby go to sleep in your arms too often, as she'll start to expect your arms to be there every time she wants to go to bed, which is what's known in child psychology circles as a 'crutch.' Other crutches include falling asleep while watching TV, falling asleep with a specific stuffed animal, and falling asleep only while breastfeeding. What you want is for your baby to learn how to sleep on her own without you or anything else present. Here are some useful ideas for getting her to sleep:

How to get your baby to sleep

1 Look for signs that your baby is tired. She might rub her eyes, yawn, or start to get grumpy (which may include crying). If she has just finished eating and her nappy is dry, there's a good chance she wants a nap.

2 Rather than just putting your baby in her cot or bassinet and leaving the room – a move that will create a crying baby and some say an emotionally scarred baby with an abandonment complex and a problem with trust – put on some soft music and start to rock your baby in your arms. Rocking chairs are great for this.

3 Before the baby falls asleep in your arms, just as she's about to drop off, place her in her cot.

4 If it's cold in the house or outside, consider warming up the sheets in your baby's bed with a warm towel before putting her down. Cold sheets can be jarring.

5 If she just won't sleep in her cot, try walking her around the block in a pushchair that folds down flat. Putting her in a carrier that holds her close to your body and going for a walk also works. Other options are a vibrating chair or self-swinging swing, which can work wonders for sleepy babies.

6 If all else fails, put the baby in her car seat and go for a drive.

Bedtime stories

A bedtime story can become a really precious and much anticipated part of your child's evening routine. Not only is it a wonderful opportunity for some physical bonding, as you cuddle together while you read, it is also an extremely effective way to help your child wind down after her busy day in readiness for sleep.

Get comfortable

Once she has got her pyjamas on, has brushed her teeth and taken a last trip to the bathroom, let her snuggle up with you on the bed and share a story. It is a lovely way to end the day. If you have more than one child, sit between them so that they can each see the book. Otherwise you will be interrupted as they jostle to get a better view.

Keep it fun

Don't choose a book that is way beyond their comprehension, keep it at their level. Of course, bedtime stories have a part to play in your child's ongoing education, but above all they should be fun. If you turn it into a chore they'll become bored and frustrated. If they can read the odd word or even whole sentences, ask them for their help in reading now and then. Let them ask questions about the story or discuss what is happening in the pictures so that the experience encourages interaction.

Keep it fresh

Children will often ask for the same favourite story night after night, and that is fine. It is reassuring and familiar for them, even if it starts to become a little repetitive for you. Maybe once or twice a week you could try something new. This is made somewhat easier if their favourite story is one of a series or one with a particular character that appears in other stories too. Give the characters funny voices or mannerisms and play to the crowd. Lose your inhibitions, your children will love it. It's best not to get them too wound up though or you'll completely defeat the object of trying to help them sleep!

Know when to stop

The point of reading a story is that you do want them to go to sleep eventually. Agree beforehand how much you will read so there are no disappointments when it is time for lights out. It is important that age-appropriate elements occur in their stories, but be careful of scary stories. Remember how vivid children's imaginations can be – you don't want to end up soothing away nightmares all night long. Try to end the story on a high note.

Top story tips

Do
- → Read just before lights out.
- → Choose something age-appropriate.
- → Get them involved.

Don't
- → Get them overexcited!
- → Make it too long.
- → Read scary stories.

The first day at school

The first day at school can be a worrying and scary time for children and for Mum too. There are several things you can do to reassure your child and help you both get through it.

Visit

Every school will invite new pupils to visit at least once in the term before they start, to help the children familiarise themselves with their classroom and teachers. You can help by talking things through before and afterwards, making sure that on these preliminary visits your child finds out the answers to any important questions that may be bothering her (like 'Where is the loo?').

Uniforms and kit

It might seem like you have weeks and weeks, but try and buy early. Give yourself plenty of time in case you need to order items that have been sold out. Mark every single item with your child's name – not just uniform but plimsolls, lunch boxes, pencils and hairbands – anything you ever want to see again. Unless they are clearly labelled they won't be returned if they get lost.

Practice

There are lots of things you can practice at home, so that your child feels more confident about managing on her own at school. It will also reassure you that she'll be able to survive without you for

a few hours. Getting dressed and managing to do up her shoes unaided will stop her feeling nervous when it comes to changing at school. If she is to have a cooked lunch at school, try and introduce a variety of foods beforehand so that nothing will surprise her. You might even consider doing a practice school run, so that you know exactly how long it is going to take, which route works best, and you can prepare yourself for the hectic school time rush.

The night before
Get everything ready the night before so you both feel prepared and there is no last minute rush in the morning. Put all the necessary kit in the right bags – PE kit, pencils and books, or anything else your child might need, and leave the bags by the front door. Lay out her school uniform ready on a chair and make a packed lunch if needed and leave it in the fridge. Knowing that you are physically prepared for the big day should help you both go to bed a little more relaxed.

Saying goodbye
Don't hang about. Make your 'Goodbye' brief. Tell her you love her and that you'll see her at the end of the school day. Show her where the big hand and the little hand of the clock will be when it is home time, and reassure her that you will be there right on time to pick her up (and then don't be late!). Hand her over. Don't look back. Go home and have a stiff gin.

Helping with homework

Helping your child with your homework can be potentially a very stressful situation, for both Mum and child. It helps to establish some ground rules early on to make homework a good habit. The following suggestions are suitable whatever your child's age.

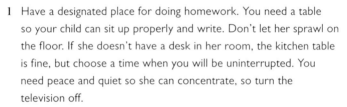

1　Have a designated place for doing homework. You need a table so your child can sit up properly and write. Don't let her sprawl on the floor. If she doesn't have a desk in her room, the kitchen table is fine, but choose a time when you will be uninterrupted. You need peace and quiet so she can concentrate, so turn the television off.

2　Have a regular time when you always sit down together. It is not a good idea to impose it on her the minute she arrives back from school; she needs to unwind from her day a little first. However, don't leave it until the last minute just before bedtime, as she will be tired then.

3　Make sure you have everything you need to hand before you start – pencils, rubbers, rulers, geometry equipment etc., so she doesn't have any excuse to get up and break her concentration.

4　Be patient and take it slowly. You are there as a guiding hand, not as a teacher. Take it at her pace and encourage her to work out the answers for herself. Have a chat with her form teacher at the start of term and ask for guidance about how long your child should be studying each evening. It might help to put a clock on the table and set the alarm for the allotted time, so you can both see that the end is in sight.

5 Don't do it all for her. If it's taking a long time it can be tempting to take over instead of taking the time to explain it and get it right on her own, but while doing a ten-year-old's homework may make you feel super-smart, it's not really going to encourage her academic progress.

6 Whatever you do, don't get cross! If she really doesn't understand her homework, keep calm. Try and avoid turning it into a battleground. Explain it as gently and clearly as you can (if you understand it!) and if she still can't complete the work after a good attempt, let her stop. Tell her that it is perfectly OK not to understand things, but she must talk to her teacher about it the following day. This often has the desired effect of weeding out genuine confusion from laziness or avoidance. If your child is very young, you might offer to speak to the teacher about it yourself.

7 Reward her with a biscuit or a tasty treat when it is finished, and however she does, try and end on a positive note. Tell her you are proud of her achievements and her willingness to give it her best efforts.

8 If your child gets weekend homework, try and get it finished on Friday evening, or you will forget about it.

Cooking quick meals

There are some evenings when you simply won't have time to spend an hour preparing a meal, or two hours waiting for it to slow roast in the oven. You need to make sure you have some quick meal plans in mind for such occasions. It helps if most of the ingredients for your quick meal plans are common items you might already have to hand in your storecupboard or fridge. Then if you have to put together a last-minute meal in a hurry, you'll already have everything to hand. So keep your cupboard well-stocked with some basic goods, such as dried pasta, rice and herbs, and canned beans and fruits, and remember to replace them as you use them so that you'll always be able to throw together a meal at the drop of a hat.

Remember, fast food does not have to mean junk, unappetising, highly calorific and laden with fat. When you are short of time you can easily cook up some quick meals for your family which look and taste great, and can even be good for you.

Top ideas for quick meals

> ↦ **Pasta**. Keep some dried pasta in the store cupboard as a quick pasta meal is easy to put together and it can always be a fall-back plan. Try adding some chopped ham or bacon, fresh tomatoes and grated cheese, or try stirring through some pesto and crème fraîche and top with parmesan.
> ↦ **Pan-fried steak**. Just serve with fresh green salad and new potatoes. Add a dash of red wine to the pan and stir about to make the most of the meat juices for a quick gravy.

→ **Chicken breast.** There are many options for turning chicken breasts into quick and tasty dishes. Do make sure the chicken is cooked all the way through before serving. Slice a pocket in the breast and pop in some sun dried tomatoes, a spoonful of pesto or cream cheese. Wrap it all up in bacon, and just leave it cooking. Or try homemade chicken nuggets; cut the chicken into pieces, cover with milk or beaten egg and then coat with breadcrumbs. Baking them in the oven is the healthy option, but you can also deep-fry them.

→ **Spanish-style omelette.** Chop some peppers and onions, spicy sausage and cooked potatoes, combine in a pan and after five minutes pour over a couple of beaten eggs. For a vegetarian option try replacing the sausage with mushrooms.

→ **Stir fry.** This is one of the quickest and easiest dinners to do. Fry strips of beef (although pork, chicken and prawns also work well with stir fries) with onions, garlic, ginger, peppers, broccoli and noodles. Add soy sauce and a dash of sherry.

→ **Jacket potatoes.** Bake them in the oven until crisp on the outside and soft in the middle. Top with whatever you fancy, whether it's cheese, chilli con carne or just a bit of butter.

Healthy foods

Keeping an eye on your family's diet and making sure everyone is eating well can seem like a difficult task, but it does not have to be difficult or expensive to cook healthy meals for your family. You can make an immediate difference to everyone's health by getting into the habit of cooking without adding extra fat or salt and using one of the following healthy methods.

Healthy cooking methods

→ **Grilling.** This is an ideal way to cook meat, fish and vegetables. A wire rack raises the food under a direct heat source, so that the fat can drain away.

→ **Poaching.** Food is gently simmered in a small amount of liquid like wine, water, milk or stock. This is a perfect method for cooking succulent pieces of fish. Use a lid to prevent too much of the liquid evaporating and you can then use the remaining liquid to make soups and sauces.

→ **Steaming.** If you steam vegetables instead of boiling them, they retain more nutrients. It is not expensive to purchase a proper steamer unit or a bamboo basket especially for the purpose, but you really don't need special equipment to steam food. A colander or sieve resting on top of a saucepan half full of boiling water will serve adequately. If you can't find a lid to fit, fashion one out of tin foil to stop the steam escaping.

→ **Stir-frying**. This method works best in a wok or large-bottomed frying pan. Bite-size pieces of food are stirred rapidly over a moderately high heat using a very small amount of oil.

→ **Baking and roasting**. These can be healthy methods too. Brush a little oil on to fish, poultry or vegetables, wrap in a loose parcel of tin foil and bake on a tray in the oven. Use a rack for roasting large joints of meat to let the fat drain away.

Fruit and vegetables

Even when trying your very best to provide your family with healthy foods, it's not always easy to convince children to eat what's good for them. Many children are suspicious of vegetables, and the idea of a piece of fruit as a snack probably won't appeal quite as much as a cookie, or anything else that is equally bad for them.

However, there are ways to encourage your child to eat foods that are good for her. If you can make food interesting, she will be much more inclined to eat it. Turn it into a little game ('Open wide, here comes the aeroplane!'), try cutting the vegetables into shapes to engage your child's interest and encourage her to eat fruit as a dessert as often as you can.

Soup for sick days

There is nothing more comforting than a bowl of Mother's nourishing homemade soup. When your children are feeling ill or just a little bit under the weather, a soothing broth is nutritious while being gentle on upset tummies.

How to make quick and easy chicken broth

You will need

- Half an onion, peeled and diced
- A knob of butter
- 1.25 litres (2 pints) chicken stock
- 3 carrots, peeled and diced
- One chicken breast, left whole
- Bay leaf
- Salt and pepper

1 In a large saucepan, sweat the onion in a little butter on a low heat for five minutes.
2 Add the stock, carrots, whole chicken breast and bay leaf, season with salt and pepper and simmer on a medium heat until the meat and vegetables are cooked through, about 20 minutes.
3 Remove the chicken breast from the pan and tear into pieces.
4 Toss half the chicken pieces back into the pan and using a handheld blender, blitz everything until smooth.
5 Add the remaining chicken pieces, heat through again and serve with warm bread.

For a variation on this recipe and a more substantial chunky soup, do not use a blender, and add a selection of extra vegetables such as leeks, sweetcorn, and potatoes, or pasta shapes. Alternatively, for a quick tomato soup as a vegetarian option, leave out the chicken and carrots, and use two tins of chopped tomatoes.

Baking a pie

The smell of a freshly baked pie is guaranteed to win the attention of your family – just don't leave it unattended for long! A pie is a perfect dessert all year round, as you can use whatever fruits are in season, from blackberries to apples, and in all sorts of combinations. You can get started with this peach pie, and see where you go from there.

How to make a peach pie

You will need

- Ready-to-roll shortcrust pastry
- A rolling pin
- A ceramic, glass pyrex or metal pie dish
- A fork
- 4–5 large peaches
- Water
- A saucepan
- 110 g (1/2 cup) of sugar
- Cornstarch

1 Preheat the oven to 190° C (375°F).
2 Roll out the pastry and fit it over your pie plate, trimming off any excess pastry.
3 Prick the pastry all over with a fork before baking it in an oven until golden.
4 Meanwhile, blanch the peaches by putting them in a jug of boiling water for about 20 seconds, then emptying them out and pouring cold water over them. This loosens the skin so that they are easy to peel.
5 Cut the peaches into slices and discard the stones.

6   Place all but one of the sliced
    peaches in a saucepan together
    with a cup of water. Keep one
    peach in reserve for later.

7   Heat on a medium heat,
    mashing occasionally with a potato
    masher or fork. Add the sugar, turn
    down heat and simmer for about 10 minutes.

8   In a cup, mix 3 tablespoons of cornstarch with 160 ml
    (2/3 cup) of cold water.

9   Bring the fruit mixture back to the boil and slowly stir in the
    cornstarch-and-water mixture.

10 Cook until the mixture is clear and thickened. Take off the heat
    and allow to cool slightly.

11 Decorate the base of the pie crust with the last peach, which
    you've peeled and sliced but not cooked.

12 Pour the cooled fruit mixture over the top and refrigerate.
    The pie-to-die-for is ready to serve whenever you and your
    guests (you mean you're going to share?!) want to eat.

Sweet treats

While it's a good idea to make sure your family eat healthy food most of the time, the occasional sweet treat can be fun to make – not to mention tasty to eat!

How to make cupcakes

You will need

→ A food processor
→ 125 g (4 oz) unsalted butter, softened
→ 125 g (4 oz) caster sugar
→ 125 g (4 oz) self-raising flour
→ 1/4 teaspoon vanilla extract
→ 2–3 tablespoons of milk
→ 12-bun muffin tin lined with muffin papers

For the icing

→ Food colouring
→ 250 g (8 oz) icing sugar
→ Decorations such as glacé cherries or miniature sweets

1 Preheat the oven to 200°C (390°F).
2 Put all the ingredients except the milk in a food processor and mix together well. When the mixture is smooth, pulse the processor while adding milk down the funnel until the mixture is a soft, fluffy consistency.
3 Share out the mixture equally between the muffin cases using a spoon. Put the cases in the oven and bake for 15–20 minutes, or

until the cakes are golden on top and cooked all the way through.

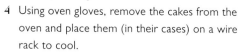

4 Using oven gloves, remove the cakes from the oven and place them (in their cases) on a wire rack to cool.

5 To decorate them, cut off the mounded tops of each cake so that you have a flat surface. Top with whatever colour and whichever decorations you want to use. You can make your own icing by mixing the icing sugar with a tablespoon or so of hot water (or you can use butter to make butter icing) and adding the food colouring of your choice.

6 To add a bit of interest to your cupcakes, you could turn them into butterfly cakes. Cut off the tops with a sharp knife and put them to one side. Make butter icing by beating together a quantity of soft, unsalted butter with twice the amount of sifted icing sugar until the sugar is all blended in. Add food colouring of your choice, or if you want different coloured cupcakes, divide the icing into batches and add a different colour to each one. Put a large blob of icing in the middle of the cake. Take the tops you sliced off and cut them in half, then place them on top of the icing to resemble butterfly wings.

How to make homemade ice cream

Ice cream is always a favourite sweet treat, particularly in hot weather. Of course there is an endless range to choose from at the supermarket, and on an average evening this is generally a better course of action. But if you have a special occasion or are feeling adventurous in the kitchen, you can also make your own.

You will need

- → 4 eggs (separated)
- → 85 g (3 oz) sugar
- → 285 ml (1/2 pint) of whipping cream
- → Vanilla essence (or preferred flavouring)

1 Whisk the egg yolks in a bowl until blended.
2 Whisk the egg whites in a separate bowl until they form soft peaks.
3 Whisk in the sugar, a teaspoonful at a time. The whites will become stiffer as the sugar is added.
4 Blend in the egg yolks until no streaks or colour remain.
5 Whisk the cream until it forms soft peaks and then fold into the mixture.
6 Add a few drops of vanilla essence, if desired.
7 Turn the mixture out into a large container, cover and freeze until solid. While freezing, stir every 30 minutes to stop ice crystals forming.

Top ideas for making ice lollies

On a sunny day, another great alternative to ice cream is an ice lolly. And the best of it is that if you invest in a set of moulds, you can use a variety of fruit to make tasty and healthy treats.

If you don't have ice lolly moulds, try sticking a toothpick into the centre of strawberries, raspberries or chunks of banana and freezing them on a tray for an ice lolly with a difference. (You can store them in bags once they've frozen if space is an issue.) For mini ice lollies, pour some fruit juice into ice cube trays. Partially freeze them, place toothpicks in the centre of each cube and then freeze fully.

» Pour apple, orange, mango or any other fruit juice straight into moulds and freeze.
» Got any stewed fruit left over from another recipe? Freeze it in a mould for a great variation.
» Blend your favourite fruit (strawberries work well) with yoghurt and a dash of fruit juice, and freeze in moulds for a delicious 'milk' popsicle.
» Make up some jelly and pour into moulds and freeze.
» Blend some watermelon (with the seeds removed) with orange juice and water and freeze the mixture.

Practical Mum

+ Decorating a nursery

+ Stopping thumbsucking

+ Handling temper tantrums

+ Mending clothes

+ Choosing a school

Multi-tasking is one of the secrets to handling the practical side of motherhood. It soon becomes second nature to most mums — we can do lots of things at the same time, because we have to! There are many new practical considerations you need to think about as a mother. Do you have a nursery? Is your home safe for your child? How do you choose a school for your child? In this chapter you'll learn plenty of sensible advice on getting organised and managing your time, and tips on dealing with challenging behaviour, housekeeping and budgeting will help you win your Practical Mum badge with ease.

Preparing a nursery

A nursery is an important part of preparing for a baby. Your little one will take over your life and most likely your home, but creating a nursery early on can help contain the chaos. It can serve as a cupboard of sorts until the baby makes his appearance. When friends and family shower you with baby gifts, they can pile up and take over your home if you don't have a space already prepared for them.

If the cost of all new gear gives you the jitters, consider other options. Basinettes and baby clothes can be useful one month, but obsolete the next once the baby grows out of them. Ask friends with older children to lend you their second-hand gear. Or check out second-hand shops or online auctions for this kind of equipment.

Decorating the nursery

No matter if it's a boy or a girl, these creative motifs can make any nursery a magical place for your baby. If you don't have a lot of artistic talent, use stencils or paint quotes from your favourite childhood books on the walls to keep your baby – and you – inspired.

Nursery themes

Jungle	Paint friendly lions, tigers, elephants and monkeys peeking through tall grasses and bushes.
Nautical	Paint your walls a deep blue and dot one wall with waves, sailboats and a lighthouse.
Forest	Place a couple of faux trees (or potted trees) in the corners that you can sit under with your baby when reading books.
Garden	Paint bright big blooms on the walls to create a stimulating environment.
Outer space	Aliens are always nifty.
Beach	If you're not averse to cleaning, how about an indoor sandbox or a beach umbrella?
Zoo	Large stuffed animals create a wild menagerie.
Circus	Paint elephants, clowns, acrobats, lion tamers and a ringmaster on the walls; paint a big top on the ceiling.
Under the sea	Paint sea creatures, both real and imaginary, on the wall; add a fish mobile and an aquarium.

Child safety

When a new baby arrives, you will find time goes very quickly. Before long your little one will be toddling and exploring. Suddenly every sharp corner, the staircase, a slippery floor all become a potential health hazard to your intrepid toddler. You need to be prepared and put child safety measures in place before he gets to this stage.

Keep things out of reach

Many everyday items are potentially dangerous for your child; cleaning materials and household chemicals should be locked away, as should medicines, knives, cigarette lighters, matches and alcohol.

The kitchen is an especially dangerous place for small children: saucepan handles can be pulled off the stove; electrical flexes trailing from irons or kettles are also in danger of being pulled down; likewise, hot drinks left on the edge of a table can lead to disaster. In fact, it's best just to never leave a small child unattended in the kitchen.

Always keep small items out of reach as well, as your toddler will put everything in his mouth and the danger of choking is very real. This is a particular problem if you have older children as well – some of their toys may include small pieces, made even more attractive by their bright colours, and just asking to be eaten!

Guarding your child

There are also ways to make your home safer for your child. Moulded plastic shields can be fixed on sharp corners, such as the edges of coffee tables. Special guards designed for video recorders and TVs and covers for electrical sockets will prevent little fingers fiddling where they shouldn't. Plastic gadgets are available which stop doors slamming shut and squashing little hands.

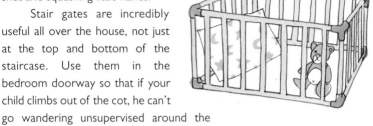

Stair gates are incredibly useful all over the house, not just at the top and bottom of the staircase. Use them in the bedroom doorway so that if your child climbs out of the cot, he can't go wandering unsupervised around the house. A playpen is also handy to restrict his wanderings, especially one that opens out and doubles as a room divider.

Safety in the garden

Don't overlook your outdoor space. Ensure all fencing and gates are secure, especially if your garden is near a road. Look out for loose panels, exposed nails, uneven paving slabs or broken stones on pathways and patios. All dangerous tools and chemicals should be kept locked away.

Trim back any prickly plants and check to see if you have any poisonous ones growing where children might come into contact with them. Ponds are a particular point of concern. Fit a pond guard (a wire mesh that sits just below the water line) or fill it in. Water and toddlers don't mix well.

Bath times

Nappy wipes can only clean a baby so much, which is why you'll need to wash him with soap and water every few days. In the first weeks, a sponge bath will work fine. Then, as soon as the umbilical cord or a boy's circumcision has completely healed, you can fill up a tiny bath. It's always good to give your baby a bath before bedtime. With an evening routine of feeding and then bathing, there's a strong chance he'll be out before you finish the first verse of 'The Wheels on the Bus'. Over the years, this will become a ritual that they will look forward to.

How to bathe your baby

1   Whatever you plan to bathe your baby in should be filled with warm water. Use the inside of your wrist or forearm to feel the temperature (hands are often insensitive to water that's too hot). The water should be only slightly warmer than body temperature. A baby's skin is very sensitive, so take care.

2   If your house tends to be cold, either from a strong air-conditioner or a weak heater, consider wrapping your baby in a towel or blanket before lowering him into the water.

3   Gently lower the baby into the water and ALWAYS hold him with one hand and arm, making sure to support his head. Do not leave a small baby alone in even the smallest amount of water. If you've forgotten something, take

your baby with you (just be sure to wrap him in a dry towel before you do).

4 Use your other hand and a washcloth to wipe your baby's face very gently. Clean his eyes by wiping from near the nose to the outer corners, being careful to catch any little bits of sleep. Wipe behind his ears and in the folds of the ears. It's okay to use cotton swabs on the external parts of a baby's ear, but never put a swab in the ear canal. This can damage the extra-sensitive eardrum.

5 Wash the rest of his body with a washcloth and soap, starting with the neck and working your way down. If it's cold and the baby is wrapped in a towel, uncover one section and then cover it back up as you go.

6 Lastly, use a small amount of shampoo to wash your baby's hair (or in many cases, his head). You don't need to lather it up as much as you would your own hair. You'll only have to use more water to rinse it off if you do that, which provides more chances for you to get water and soap in your baby's face and eyes. Rinse by tilting your baby's head back and slowly pouring water over it so that the water runs from front to back, away from his little eyes. Take your baby out of the bath, wrap him in a dry towel, and, if the towel has a hood, put the hood over his head. Hold him close to let him warm up before putting on a nappy and some clothes.

Changing nappies

Changing nappies will become a pretty regular feature in your life when a new baby arrives. You'll find that pretty quickly you'll be able to swap a dry one for a wet one with your eyes closed.

If your baby is getting nappy rash and getting fussy because of it, it may be that you're not changing his nappies often enough. Many paediatricians suggest changing nappies eight to ten times a day – or even double that for cloth nappies.

1 Before you get started, make sure all the things you need – nappies, wipes, ointments and nappy pail – are within easy reach. You should never leave a baby unattended, so you'll want to keep one hand on him at all times. Even the smallest babies have been known to jerk suddenly, and you do *not* want a baby to fall.
2 Lay your baby gently on a changing table, floor or any other firm surface. Make sure the surface is covered with some kind of washable blanket or pee-proof material.
3 Take off the nappy by loosening the fasteners on each side.
4 Lift your baby's rear end off the surface by holding his tiny feet in one hand. At the same time, pull the nappy away from his bottom.
5 If you're dealing with more than just a wet nappy, fold the front of the nappy under your baby's bottom so that everything is covered and you will have a place to rest the dirty bottom while you fish for a nappy wipe. Don't let go of your baby's feet or you'll have more than a bottom to clean. Also, if you have a boy, you'd be smart to cover his penis with a cloth while all this is going on or you can count on getting peed on.

6 Gently clean your baby by wiping from front to back with a baby wipe or a soft, warm, wet cloth. This is particularly important for baby girls so that you avoid the possibility of spreading infections. Do a thorough job and be sure to remove all faeces.

7 Though our parents may have used talcum powder on our young bottoms, it is frowned upon these days because babies can inhale the dust, which can lead to respiratory problems. Studies have also linked it to ovarian cancer in women. Most paediatricians recommend using a generous amount of nappy ointment instead. It serves as a protective barrier if your baby has nappy rash and it will keep moisture away from the skin.

8 When you've cleaned up and applied any ointment, hold your baby's feet in one hand, lift his bottom off the surface and slide a fresh nappy under it.

9 Fold the front of the nappy between your baby's legs, over his front and fasten one side of the nappy and then the other. Make sure the nappy fits snugly around your baby's hips and that the tape or Velcro isn't cutting into his skin.

Potty training

There are all sorts of methods espoused by experts to achieve successful potty training. These range from parents training their child in just one day, to encouraging the child to take as long as he needs until he decides to do it all by himself.

The most sensible approach seems to be somewhere between the two. The success and speed of potty training is greatly determined by the attitude of the parents, so how you go about dealing with this issue makes all the difference.

Knowing when to start

It's not always easy knowing when to start potty training. As a general rule, children are being potty trained much later now than they were 20 years ago. Obviously it doesn't pay to start too young, before your child has learnt to recognise the feeling that he needs to relieve himself. However, you don't want to leave it too late, or soiling and wetting may become a difficult habit to break. Each child is an individual case, but around two and a half years seems to be the average age to start.

It is a good idea to start potty training when you have a few weeks uninterrupted at home. The holidays are the best time, when your child is not in daycare.

No more nappies!

Introduce the potty early on so your child can become familiar with it, maybe at bath times. While your child is undressed, encourage him to sit on the potty every evening. On the rare occasion you get a

If you are having trouble keeping your child on the potty, give him a toy that he can play with, read a book with him, or sing his favourite songs and nursery rhymes to keep him occupied and distract his attention away from the potty. If he is kept entertained he will be less restless.

winning result, make a huge fuss of your child and congratulate him with wild applause.

The next stage is to introduce the potty at regular times. The best way to do this is by working out your child's natural rhythms and producing the potty in advance, at the same times every day. Make sure that the potty is always to hand and eventually he will start to ask for it himself.

Your child knows, quite rightly, that it is OK to relieve himself when he is wearing his nappy, so it is sensible to dress your child in proper underpants from now on so he is not confused.

Positive thinking

Keep praising your child, tell him how grown up he is and perhaps reward him with a treat after each successful sitting. Accidents are inevitable, but try not to lose your patience. Making a fuss only causes your child to become nervous and anxious, which causes more accidents. If your child does make a mess, play it down. Assure him that it does not matter and immediately sit him on the potty. It may be too late, but it reinforces the message. If you keep it positive, potty training does not have to be a stressful experience for you or your child.

Exercising your baby

Exercising your baby is a good way to spend time with him while promoting good co-ordination and muscle development. A 10-minute session a day is all it takes, and you can do it while changing his nappy.

Exercises to do with your baby

1   Babies will instinctively hold onto your finger when you place it in their hands. This can strengthen arm and hand muscles.

2   At about three months old, your baby will begin to be able to grip things. Help him out by handing him a rattle. When he drops it, hand it to him again.

3   At about three or four months, he will have control over neck muscles and should be able to hold his head up. You can promote stomach strength by holding his hands and pulling him up to a sitting position.

4   Bicycle his legs by placing him on his back, holding his feet, and gently moving his legs back and forth so he's making cycling motions. This also helps relieve stomach pain associated with gas or colic.

5   Six-month-old babies start to have good control over their arms and grasping motions. Lay a six-month-old baby on his back under a 'baby gym' or homemade mobile and help him reach out and grab the hanging objects above him.

6   Take your baby for a swim with you. When he gets in the pool he'll splash and kick, and be very active.

Teach your kids to swim

Most children are not physically able to swim proficiently until they are about five years old and can start lessons with a professional swimming instructor, however there is plenty you can do before then to get them confident in the water.

Bath time practice

The bath tub is a great place to start, but never, ever leave your kids unattended in the bath. Children can drown in as little as 2 inches of water. Encourage them to splash and get water on their faces. When you are hair washing, be brisk and matter-of-fact about it. The idea is to help children feel comfortable in water and that getting water in your ears and eyes does not have to be frightening.

Sink or swim

1   At about the age of four, you can move on to kicking practice in the pool.
2   Make sure he is wearing his water wings before getting in.
3   Get your child to hold on to the side of the pool and stretch out his legs behind. At first you will need to support his torso with your arm so that his body floats in a horizontal position.
4   Get him to practice kicking until he is confident enough to do it while you hold his hands and walk the width of the pool.
5   Encourage him to swim short distances to you unaided. He'll be swimming like a fish in no time.

Stop thumb-sucking

Thumb-sucking is a child's natural way of comforting themselves. It is quite common in small children and shouldn't be seen as a problem. However, some children continue this habit until they are much older and it can be a source of worry to their parents.

What to do if you are worried

If you are concerned that your child's thumb-sucking may be symptomatic of a more distressing problem, it is wise to get him checked out by the paediatrician. Some experts believe it can cause dental and speech problems, but although it is a habit that can embarrass the parents, it is normally no more sinister than that.

Small steps

Introducing a 'no thumbs' rule during conversation or at the table is a good way to encourage your child to stop. You could also gently suggest that as your child is growing up now, he might like to limit his thumb-sucking to bedtimes.

Positive non-intervention

Shouting, punishing your child or drawing negative attention to his thumb-sucking, will only make him feel agitated and self-conscious, which will make him want to suck his thumb. Usually he will stop gradually of his own accord, not long after starting school (due, in part, to the inevitable teasing he receives from his peers) – so it might be better to ignore this behaviour and let your child stop thumb-sucking when he is ready.

Getting your kids to bed . . .

The secret to calm and stress-free bedtimes is in establishing a regular routine from the earliest age and sticking to it. If your child knows what to expect each night, he will be comforted by the familiarity of the evening ritual and will understand that it signifies the end of the day and time for sleep. Children do often protest at bedtime and try to come up with excuses to stay up a little later, so be prepared to avoid the most common ones.

But I'm not tired!

It helps if your child is tired at bedtime! If he is a pre-schooler it might be an idea to restructure his naptime, making sure that he doesn't sleep for too long or too late in the afternoon. Exercise also helps, especially for older children. Let them enjoy plenty of fun and games in the fresh air or get into the habit of going for a walk after school each day.

But I'm hungry!

Make sure he has been fed. If he has an early supper, consider giving him a carbohydrate snack and a glass of warm milk before bed. A full tummy will help him feel sleepy and also means you won't have to bring him a snack half an hour after you have tucked him in.

. . . and out of bed

If you put your child to bed at a sensible time each evening, getting up in the morning should not pose a problem. Most young children can't wait to begin the day and will bound out of bed with all the enthusiasm of the young. However, as they get older, especially when they reach adolescence, getting up in the morning can become a more difficult issue.

Routine

However old your child is, an established and consistent bedtime routine will help your child feel rested and ready to start a new day. Getting enough sleep is vital. Don't be afraid to set a regular bedtime for older children. Watch how many extra-curricular activities he may be doing during the week and limit social events to the weekend.

Wakey wakey!

Make mornings as calm as possible. Get him to lay out his kit for school before he goes to sleep, so that he doesn't wake up and feel pressured to get organised first thing. Don't make it easy for him to roll over and go back to sleep either. Suggest that he puts his alarm clock on the opposite side of the room so that he actually has to get out of bed to turn it off. Similarly, if you take him a cup of coffee first thing, be sure to leave it where he has to get up to drink it!

Make children tidy their rooms

It is as well to establish some ground rules from the earliest age so that your child learns good habits. If you teach your child what is expected of him from the beginning, keeping his bedroom tidy is less likely to become a running battle.

Get children involved

A toddler can pick up his dirty clothes and deposit them into the laundry basket. Once he gets to primary school age, he will be able to smooth over his duvet and make his bed neat. When you fold the clean laundry, ask him to put his clothes away in his drawers. Delegate these jobs as soon as your child is old enough to handle them.

Stay on top of storage

It is worth being quite strict about toys. Do not allow your child to get out any more than two boxes at a time. He may want to play with his cars and his bricks at the same time, but if he then decides to play with his train set, he must put away something else first. This does help prevent the chaos of toys that threatens to take over the bedroom floor and takes ages to sort out and put away.

Provide your child with appropriate storage. You can't expect him to put away his clothes and toys if there are not enough shelves or containers to keep things in. Label everything, not just his toy boxes, so he knows exactly where jumpers and trousers or socks and underclothes belong. For very young children who cannot read, try cutting out a picture of the item from a magazine and using it instead of a written label. This is something fun you could do together which would encourage him to take responsibility for the tidiness of his own things.

Tidying up at the end of the day should be part of your child's routine. Make it fun and it will not be a chore. Have races as to who can clean up their corner of the room first, or compete to see who can toss the most bricks into the box.

Teenage terrors

Of course, encouraging older children to keep their rooms tidy is a different ball game altogether, but if you have always encouraged tidiness and got your kids into the habit, it is half the battle.

It is worth making a new set of rules for teenagers, for instance, dirty clothes that don't make it into the laundry basket, don't get washed. Try and keep positive. If you constantly berate your child for the state of his room, it will become an area of contention. Instead, praise him when it is looking clean and tidy.

If his room is looking a little babyish now he is growing up, consider a makeover. Let him choose a new colour scheme, redecorate and buy some co-ordinating bed linen. Make his room something he can be proud of and he'll want to keep it clean and tidy.

Deal with a fussy eater

Most young children will go through a stage of fussy eating at some point or another. Although it can be a source of worry and irritation to the parents, it normally resolves itself after a period of time. Obviously if you are concerned that your child has developed a serious eating problem, take him to see his paediatrician, but as long as your child is meeting his developmental milestones for height and weight, it really is better not to make a big issue about your child's eating habits. To avoid turning mealtimes into battle zones, there are a few things that parents can do to to encourage their child to eat a healthy and varied diet.

Laying down rules

Establish some rules for family meal times and adhere to them. Try and establish a routine – eat at roughly the same time every day, sit up at the table as a family and turn off the TV. It is fine not to like everything, but your child should at least *try* everything on their plate.

Balance and structure

Portion sizes often cause parents undue worry, especially if children do not seem to be eating enough. Young children need to eat frequently, so give them three well-spaced meals and two snacks daily. Only give them water at mealtimes if possible, as otherwise they tend to fill up on milk or juice and will not finish their food. Limit sugar-laden, refined products and encourage your children to enjoy natural, unprocessed foods as far as possible. Stick to these guidelines and your children will naturally eat enough to satisfy their daily needs, and you will be reassured that they are eating a balanced nutritious diet.

Added interest

Children are much more likely to have an interest in food and an open attitude to new tastes if they are included in the preparation of meals. Let them help you decide the week's menus and suggest their favourite meals. Let them help peel, chop and slice. Get them to set the table or even play at being your 'waiter'. You could take this a stage further and even let them have a tiny plot in the garden in which to grow their very own mini-crops of vegetables. Children are suddenly more interested in carrots and beans if they have grown them themselves!

Top tips for fussy eaters

Do

 ✦ Establish a routine and rules for meals and snacks.
 ✦ Offer three balanced meals and two snacks daily.
 ✦ Serve only water at mealtimes.

Don't

 ✦ Let them fill up on drinks before a meal.
 ✦ Serve sugary processed foods regularly.
 ✦ Make a big issue about his eating habits.

Tantrums and sibling rivalry

Temper tantrums are a young child's response to an ever-changing world in which they are still learning where the boundaries lie. It is natural for children to want to assert their independence, but they require strict and defined guidelines for their safety and development.

Ignore their behaviour

You will find that if you ignore the tantrum your child will quickly learn that it is not an effective way to get your attention. Don't shout or enter negotiations, it will only prolong the tantrum. Don't offer bribes, like cuddles or sweets, in an attempt to curtail the tantrum. All you are doing is rewarding bad behaviour, and children will continue to throw a tantrum if it means they get a treat.

Avoidance tactics

You can lessen the likelihood of a tantrum by giving your child plenty of warning of events. For instance, tell him that in five minutes we need to put away our toys and wash our hands for supper. He is less likely to throw a tantrum when asked to stop playing, if he knows it is coming. Try to avoid head-on conflict – if your child is doing something that you would like him to stop, try changing the subject and diverting his attention away. Roll him along in a wave of enthusiasm about a totally different activity.

Be consistent

You can help your child learn control over his behaviour if you are consistent in everything. It is important that you establish and stick to your family's own rules and that you follow through with both rewards and punishments. Realise the importance of structure and routine to your child. All these things help him feel secure in his environment. If he knows what to expect, he is less likely to react in an uncontrolled manner.

Don't forget that he will copy your own behaviour too, so set him a good example. It is important that he sees that sometimes life throws up the unexpected or a challenge. Let him see you react in a calm and measured way. Show him that shouting and screaming achieves nothing.

Sibling rivalry

Sibling rivalry is inevitable in families of more than one child. There are a number of tactics you can deploy to minimise the arguments, restore peace and calm to your home, and prevent the rivalry escalating into long-held feuds. When conflict arises, as it inevitably will from time to time, teaching your children to compromise and co-operate is much easier if you have certain family rules about behaviour that everybody understands.

Top tips for dealing with sibling rivalry

- ⋗ Praise each of their strengths – don't make comparisons.
- ⋗ Encourage individual hobbies.
- ⋗ Don't punish angry feelings, but forbid aggressive conduct.
- ⋗ Let them sort it out themselves when they can.
- ⋗ Get ready to step in when they can't.
- ⋗ Encourage group behaviour by giving group rewards.

Organise your time

Various time management systems have been
developed for busy people, but it doesn't
have to be complicated – it just needs to
work for you. A simple notebook, pocket
diary and wall calendar is really all you
need to organise your time.

Notebook
Use your notebook to run two lists. The first list is your 'Daily Tasks'
– things that must be achieved today. Your second list is medium term
'To Do' items, which need to be done soon. Try setting aside ten
minutes each night when you get into bed to write your daily list for
the following day.

Wall calendar and pocket diary
Buy a large wall calendar and fix it up in the kitchen where everyone
in the family can see it. Then make a new house rule. If it isn't written
on the calendar, it won't happen! Encourage everyone to write down
all their commitments, appointments, meetings and so forth. This
means you will always know who needs to be doing what and when.

Achievable goals
Most mothers find that there are never enough hours in the day to
get done everything you had planned. It can be dispiriting to find that
your Daily Task list is really just the jobs you didn't complete the
previous day. Be realistic about what you can achieve and then
prioritise ruthlessly.

Budgets

Budgeting is very important once you've started a family, making sure you and your husband allow for all the expenses you're used to, such as the electricity and the rent/mortgage, and those that are new, like nappies. First you'll need to assess your financial situation, then you'll need to talk about where your financial priorities lie.

Begin by talking about what you think you can save each month, what you will spend and where the money will go. The main thing is making sure you are well aware of all the expenses you have, from fuel expenses for your car to water bills. The first step is to make a list of all the household expenses you can think of and the average cost (take a look at some old bills to estimate this). Once you know roughly what expenditure you have on a monthly basis you can factor in additional costs, work out what money you can save, and plan in little luxuries like the family holiday.

Household expenses

- ✦ Rent/mortgage
- ✦ Phone/cable/Internet
- ✦ Individual mobile phones
- ✦ Electricity
- ✦ Gas
- ✦ Water
- ✦ Local taxes
- ✦ Vehicles
- ✦ Vehicle insurance
- ✦ Home contents insurance
- ✦ Groceries
- ✦ Household items/supplies/ furnishings
- ✦ Entertainment (cinema, dinners out, etc.)
- ✦ Clothing/toiletries/grooming
- ✦ Savings/investments
- ✦ Holidays

Quick cleaning

The secret to maintaining a clean house is doing a little bit every day. If you get into the habit of swiftly tidying a room before you leave it, it will be a lot more manageable, but if you let it build up, it becomes a daunting and time-consuming task that you will find every excuse to put off. If you give all communal or public areas a swift 'going over' every day, your house will always look clean and tidy, and it really doesn't need to take more than an hour a day.

Top tips for staying on top of cleaning

→ The hallway is the first area that visitors will see, so it's important to keep this in order. Hang up hats and coats, tidy the table and wipe the mirror.

→ Fold your clothes before you climb into bed at night and put any dirty clothes straight into the laundry hamper.

→ Make your bed in the morning – it instantly returns some order to the bedroom.

→ Tidy and wipe down surfaces in all rooms regularly, especially in the kitchen after preparing food.

→ Load the dirty dishes straight into the dishwasher after mealtimes (or try to wash them by hand the same day).

→ If you sweep floors regularly in the morning, you won't need to mop them as often.

→ Keep some cleaning fluid and cloth in the bathroom cupboard and ask everyone in the family to wipe around the bath when they get out.

Delegating household jobs

Even though most mothers now work outside the home, they still end up doing most of the household chores that their husbands and even their children, could be helping with. Sometimes it feels as if it is a lot easier to just do it yourself, but if you are constantly rushed off your feet and don't ever seem to have enough hours in the day to get things done, you must learn to delegate. You must stop believing in the old maxim – 'if you want a job doing properly, do it yourself' – and start thinking about which chores could be given to which family member. Even the youngest children can do their bit to help, by picking up their dirty clothes and depositing them into the laundry basket or taking their empty dishes to the sink. Older children can lay the table and empty the dishwasher.

Learning to delegate

- → Start by drawing up a list of all the chores that need doing in a week.
- → Now go through the list and decide what you can safely delegate.
- → Ask family members to volunteer for the remaining jobs – you are more likely to get their co-operation if they feel they chose their own chores!
- → It is helpful to organise some sort of routine or rota so that everyone knows when they should be doing their jobs. This keeps things structured and in your overall control.

Mending clothes

Minor clothing repairs can be done by hand and are easy when you know how. Children's clothes are expensive, particularly when you consider how quickly your child grows out of things. Being able to mend his clothes rather than replace them, will save you a lot of money and is not at all difficult to do.

How to sew a patch

1 Cut a regular shape – a square or rectangle is most effective – from a strong fabric like corduroy or denim that has a circumference at least 5 cm wider than the area you wish to mend.
2 Turn in each edge of the patch about 2 cm, fold underneath and press firmly with a hot iron.
3 Place the patch over the torn area and pin.
4 Match your thread to the patch.
5 Use a hemming stitch to sew the patch onto the garment.

How to replace a button

1 Match your thread to the colour of the button.
2 Make one or two small stitches in the fabric where the button will sit. Pass your needle up through a hole in the button, across and down through another hole, making a small stitch in the fabric behind.
3 Repeat this process four or five times until the button feels secure.

4 Wind the thread tightly several times around the stitches behind the button and finish off with one or two small stitches in the fabric.

How to sew up a loose hem

1 With a hot iron, give the hem a good pressing.
2 Use pins vertically to secure the hem in place.
3 Match your thread to the fabric.
4 Start about 2 cm from the loose area, so that your first stitches reinforce the existing sewing.
5 Begin by securing your thread in the hem, not the skirt, making a very small stitch.
6 Then bring your needle to the skirt, using the tiniest stitches you can, picking up just one or two fibres of the fabric, so that from the right side your stitches will be invisible.
7 Pass the needle back through the hem.
8 Move along the skirt 1 cm and repeat until you have secured the hem.
9 Finish by stitching a couple of centimetres past the loose area over the existing sewing.

Laundry days

With children in the house, laundry is going to pile up at a previously unimagined rate. Not only are there more people creating dirty laundry, children have a remarkable ability to get their clothes filthy in one quick session of 'Let's make mud pies.' There's not much that can be done about that, but there are ways to tackle laundry that will make the task less daunting and avoid unnecessary washday disasters.

How to tackle laundry

❖ Understanding fabric care labels is essential to the maintenance of your clothes and other washable items. Read the manufacturer's laundry instructions and follow them. Otherwise you run the risk of shrinkage, non-fast colours running, bobbling, rips or worse.

❖ Sort your laundry into four separate piles – whites, lights, coloureds and handwash.

❖ Empty all pockets – items such as bank notes and passports are not improved by a run through the wash.

❖ Do up zips, hooks and fasteners that might snag other clothing or work loose.

❖ It is a good idea to soak or pre-treat heavily soiled items before washing, or you can end up redistributing dirt onto less soiled items in the machine.

❖ Some things are better washed inside out – particularly clothing with transfers or embroidery – but jeans will fade less quickly too if you turn them the wrong way round. The care label on the garment should indicate if it needs to be washed inside out.

To make sure your washing machine is working efficiently and lasts longer in good condition, don't overfill the machine, as clothes need enough space to be agitated correctly to facilitate the washing process. Remember to also clean the machine itself occasionally to prevent odours and blockages building up.

Stain removal

The golden rule with stains is to treat them immediately, whether on clothing, carpets, upholstery or floors. The longer you leave it, the harder it is to get the stain out.

When you find a stain, the first step is to scrape up any excess surface matter before you start the stain removal process. Attempt to blot (not rub) as much of the stain away as you can – the idea is to absorb as much of the stain as possible rather than spread it about. For the same reason, always work from the outside of the stain in.

While it is always best to use a proper stain remover designed for the job, there are some tried and tested methods for removing stubborn stains which can be surprisingly effective. They also have the added bonus of not requiring the use of strong or harmful chemicals, and are thus much kinder to the environment. If you're not sure what the stain is, the best thing to use is hot water.

Be patient with stains, whether you're using a proper stain remover or a homemade remedy. Stain removal is not an exact science, so don't expect instant miracles – the cleaning solution will take time to be effective, and you may have to repeat the treatment a few times before you see a result.

Above all, never attempt to treat a precious or irreplaceable fabric at home. Leave it to the professionals. Take it to a specialist cleaner as soon as possible.

Common stains and remedies

Blood	Soak the stain immediately in cold water – never hot water as that will set the stain. Toothpaste and milk have also been known to work.
Chewing gum	Place the item in the freezer and allow the gum to harden, and it should come off easily. Then wash according to the label. This also works for chocolate.
Ballpoint pen	Try dabbing with neat methylated spirits on a cotton wool pad, then wash as normal or rub the stain gently using a pencil eraser to fade the mark.
Cooking oil	Sprinkle talcum powder over the stain. Leave for 30 minutes and then brush the fat off. Wash as normal.
Mildew	First, take the item outside and remove the surface mildew with a stiff brush. Leave to air out in the sun. If spots remain, wash in biological detergent.
Rust	Douse the stain with salt, then pour lemon juice over it and put the garment outside in the sun. A small mark should fade after a few hours, a heavier mark may take a few days.
Mud	Allow the mud to dry, brush it off, soak the item in cool water and wash as normal. Some women used to swear by rubbing dried-on mud with a raw potato.
Perspiration	Sponge underarm perspiration with white wine vinegar, rinse, then wash as usual.

Making ironing bearable

People generally fall into two camps when it comes to ironing. They either find it mind-numbingly boring and largely unnecessary, or strangely soothing and therapeutic. If your opinion of ironing is mostly of the first attitude, do not worry, there are at least a few things you can do to lessen the pain.

Finding distractions

Set up your ironing board in front of the TV or put the radio on. Giving yourself something else to do can take your mind off the boring task at hand. If you enjoy the guilty pleasure of the occasional soap opera, you have the perfect excuse to watch them if you plan your ironing according to the TV schedule. The danger is becoming too distracted and ending up with scorch marks on your garments. If this sounds like you, try a stick and carrot system instead – divide your ironing into bundles of three items and reward yourself with a chocolate truffle every time you complete a pile.

Selective ironing

Not everything needs ironing. Sometimes giving a garment a good shake before hanging it out to dry will suffice. Heavy trousers, cords or jeans, can be shaken from the washing machine and straightened by hand while still

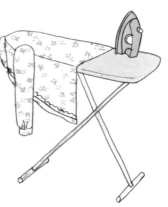

damp, then stretched over the back of a chair or hung over a door overnight to dry.

Never let anything sit in the tumble dryer after it has finished. If you take everything out when it is still warm and fold it up neatly, most things will not need ironing. Hang shirts straight onto hangers and leave them to air, and you'll be surprised how little pressing they actually require.

If you are lucky enough to have an Aga or a large range cooker, you can fold slightly damp cottons on to the closed lids of the hot plates – particularly tea-towels and pillowcases – and not a jot of ironing will be necessary.

Top tips to reduce the ironing

> → When tackling bed linen you can avoid ironing the under-sheet as it is hidden under the duvet, and only press the side of the pillowcase and duvet cover that can be seen.
> → Try investing in a couple of items of non-iron or crease-resistant clothing that you can wear in an emergency.
> → Avoid ironing anything delicate at all, particularly if it is an expensive or precious item of clothing. Use a professional cleaning service.
> → And remember – life is far too short to spend one precious moment ironing underwear or socks.

Choosing a school

Finding the right school for your child can be a daunting prospect. Your child will spend at least ten years at school, so this is one of the most important decisions you can make for him. His day-to-day happiness as well as his education and long-term future will be affected by his experience of school. He needs to be challenged and nurtured, feel safe while being encouraged to explore, and be able to access a range of academic and extra-curricular options.

As a parent, it is important that you know what to look for when choosing a school, so it is vital to do some preparation and research beforehand. Decide in advance what really matters to you, what values are important and consider the questions you would ask of a potential school.

You will want to consider the school ethos or the philosophy behind its teaching. You might want to check out what emphasis the school places on religious activities, depending on your personal beliefs. Examine the school's performance and look at exam results and education authority reports.

Once you have thought about what your child needs from a school, you are in a better position to make a judgement on a school's suitability. Arrange a number of visits. You are bound to forget something the first time you see a new place, so don't be embarrassed to make a second appointment. It helps to take a list of questions with you and a note of specific things you want to check.

Questions to ask

- ✦ What learning environment would be most suitable for your child?
- ✦ Would he benefit from a traditional environment with a disciplined structure in place or would he do better in a more relaxed setting?
- ✦ Does he have any special needs and can the school meet them?
- ✦ Are the class sizes large or small?
- ✦ What extra-curricular activities do the school offer?
- ✦ What are the facilities like and what is the staffing ratio?
- ✦ How does the school communicate with parents?
- ✦ What are the school's policies on issues like bullying, discipline and homework?

Things to look out for

- ✦ Do the buildings and grounds look clean and cared for?
- ✦ Is the library well-stocked and how often do the children get access to it?
- ✦ What are the IT provisions in the school?
- ✦ Is the food prepared freshly on the premises and how often does the menu change?
- ✦ What PE equipment and facilities are there and how much sport is timetabled?
- ✦ As well as a full body of teaching staff, are there any specialists on site, like a nurse, librarian or educational psychologist?
- ✦ What facilities are there for extra-curricular activities like drama and music?

Meet your child's teacher

Most teachers positively encourage interaction and involvement with the family of their pupils. They know that if a child is supported by parents who are actively interested in his education, he is more likely to succeed in the classroom. Effective communication with your child's teacher is essential if you are to work together to ensure your child has a positive and fulfilling school experience.

Most schools organise an evening once a year where the parents can come and discuss their child's progress. Make the effort to attend as there may be problems at school that your child has not told you about. It also shows you care about your child's education.

Preparation

To make it a constructive and useful exercise for you and your child, think about the things you would like to talk about in advance. Talk to your child before you go and ask if there are any issues he would like you to be aware of or concerns that he wants you to raise on his behalf. Make sure that you have read any reports that have been sent home and make a note of anything you want to discuss.

When you meet the teacher, be positive. If you feel she has done a good job, say so! Show an interest in the subjects your child has been learning. Ask to see some examples of your child's academic work and let the teacher talk it through with you. If anything comes up in your discussion that you want to clarify further, make a follow-up appointment for a later date.

If there are any areas of concern or issues on which you disagree with the teacher, don't be afraid to speak up. This is the perfect time to address any problems. Remain patient and polite, and try to help the teacher to come up with ways you can both work together to support your child's learning.

Questions to ask the teacher about your child

Prepare a list of questions beforehand that you know you want to ask the teacher about your child's progress and overall experience at the school, for example:

- ☆ Is he happy at school?
- ☆ What does he enjoy most in the classroom?
- ☆ What does he find most difficult?
- ☆ Does he have a positive attitude?
- ☆ In what subject areas are his strengths and weaknesses?
- ☆ Does he require extra help in any particular area?
- ☆ Has there been any great improvement or deterioration in his performance this year?
- ☆ Is his progress measurable with his peers?
- ☆ Is he making the grade in the core subjects?
- ☆ How is he doing with extra-curricular activities?
- ☆ How is he progressing socially and are there any problems with social interaction?
- ☆ Is he confident enough to speak out in class?
- ☆ Do you have any worries about his behaviour?
- ☆ What can we do at home to help his progress further?
- ☆ Are you pleased with his progress?

Organise a school run

If you live in close proximity to other parents whose children attend your child's school, it makes sense to share the dropping off and picking up.

Walking bus

School runs do not necessarily have to involve the use of a car. If you live within walking distance of your child's school, why not get together with other parents and organise a 'green' run or a 'walking bus'. Not only is this an environmentally-friendly alternative, it is also much healthier for your children, who will benefit from starting the day with some fresh air and exercise.

Finding volunteers

Due to data protection issues, schools may not be able to give you the addresses and phone numbers of parents who live in your area. You could draw up a notice asking interested parents to contact you directly, and ask the school secretary or the class teacher if you may pin it up on the noticeboard where it can be seen.

Divide each school day of the week into two trips – the drop off and the pick up – and then ask each parent which trips they would like to volunteer to do. When it comes to organising a rota, you will need to take into account how many parents are involved, when they want to do the run and how many children require transport.

Entertaining Mum

- ✤ Making play dough
- ✤ Making fancy dress costumes
- ✤ Playing car games
- ✤ Having a treasure hunt
- ✤ Making a birthday cake

So you're caring and practical . . . and now you can be fun too! There are plenty of great ideas here for activities and games to do with your children. From finger painting and throwing birthday parties to organising family outings and creating games to keep them occupied on long car journeys, life with an Entertaining Mum is never dull!

Potato printing

A gloriously messy and fun way to entertain your children, potato prints can keep them occupied for hours.

You will need
> Baking potatoes
> Newspaper
> Water-based paint in
  different colours

> Shallow trays
> Knife
> Large sheets of paper

1 First, wash the potatoes and dry them.
2 Prepare your area for painting by laying down newspaper and squeezing the paint into shallow trays.
3 Cut the potatoes in half and show your child how to dip them in the paint and press them gently on the paper.
4 Once she has got the hang of it, and if you're feeling creative, you can cut simple shapes such as stars, squares or diamonds into the potato halves.

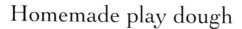

Homemade play dough

Play dough can be used for a whole range of fun games and activities with your child, and it's a great way to help strengthen young children's finger muscles as well. It's easy to make, and most of the ingredients are common storecupboard items that you're likely to already have. You will need to keep an eye on any younger children when you give them play dough, as they do have a tendency to try and eat it.

You will need
- 125g (4 oz) of plain flour
- 100g (3 1/2 oz) of salt
- 2 teaspoons of cream of tartar
- 285 ml (1/2 pint) of water
- 1 teaspoon of food colouring
- 2 teaspoons of cooking oil

1 Put the flour, salt and cream of tartar into a medium saucepan and stir together with a wooden spoon.
2 Over a medium heat, gradually stir in the water, food colouring and oil.
3 Keep stirring continually as the mixture begins to cook and forms into a sticky ball.
4 Remove from the heat. Cool for 15–30 minutes.
5 Keep in a sealed plastic bag or container in the fridge (like shop-bought dough, it will dry out if kept in the open too long).

Pasta jewellery

This is such an easy activity and perfect for a rainy day, as you are likely to have everything you need in the house already. Both boys and girls enjoy making things out of pasta. Girls can make their own jewellery fit for any little princess and boys will happily wear 'shark tooth' or Indian necklaces.

You will need
→ Dried pasta shapes (Macaroni, Penne and Rotelle are good, but any shape with a hole would be fine)
→ Twine, coloured cord or embroidery thread
→ Spray or poster paints or felt tips
→ Glitter
→ Newspaper

1 Spread the newspaper over the table and put an apron on your child, as this is likely to get messy.
2 Spread out the pasta shapes on the newspaper and let her spray them, paint them or colour them in with pens. Let her be as artistic and imaginative as she likes. Try dipping the pasta into the paint to colour just one end or try sponging paint on to get a dappled effect. With felt tips she can draw her own patterns and designs on to the larger pasta shapes.
3 While the paint is still wet, you can sprinkle them with glitter.
4 Let them dry and then thread them onto lengths of twine and knot securely. Make sure they are loose enough to slip easily over her head or wrist.

If your child is too young to handle paints and glitter, you can make the pasta more colourful by dying it. Add a teaspoon of food colouring to water, then dip the pasta pieces in for a couple of minutes until they have been stained. Remove the pasta pieces from the water and leave them to dry before threading them onto string.

Finger painting

A wonderful way to play with your child is to bring out their artistic side with finger painting and handprints. Children love the sensation of covering their hands with paint and this activity lets them do exactly that, leaving you with a collection of painted handprints that you can keep and cherish as they grow up. This is another messy activity though, so make sure to put down plenty of newspaper on your surface. Don't do this activity near carpets or other soft furnishings, and an apron is definitely advisable, or at least some old clothing.

Making handprints

1   Cover your work surface with a plastic tablecloth or sheets of newspaper, and have your child put on an apron.
2   Pour out some brightly coloured poster paint into separate trays for each colour, or mix powder paint with water in pots until it's the consistency of household paint.
3   Put out some large pieces of paper (A3 is a good size).
4   To make handprints, ask her to spread out her hand and put it into the paint, and then transfer it to the paper. Otherwise she might prefer to just dip her fingers in the paint and make her own shapes.
5   Have a container of water handy that she can rinse her hands in when changing between colours so that they don't all mix together.
6   Leave the paper on a flat surface to dry.

Making Angel fish handprints

If your children are a little old for just straight handprints, try making these Angel fish handprints instead.

You will need

- Butcher's paper, about 80–100 cm (31–40 in)
- Blue poster or powder paint
- Household sponge
- Cut-out handprints (see page 88)
- Glue stick
- Coloured felt-tip pens

1 Place the paper on a table and weigh it down at the corners.
2 Mix powder paint or dilute poster paint to a wash consistency.
3 Using the sponge, show your child how to dip it in the paint and then spread the paint onto the paper with a sweeping wave action.
4 When all the paper is covered with the blue wash, allow to dry.
5 Take one of the cut-out handprints and ask her to put glue on the non-painted side of the palm. Let her stick it anywhere on the blue painted paper.
6 Take another hand in a different colour and stick it on top of the first hand with a slight overlap, ensuring that you have the fingers all going in the same way.
7 If you have a third colour, repeat with that.
   The handprinted fingers should look like a feathery fan. Let her make several fish to fill the blue area.
8 Show her how to use pens to make eyes on the fish.
9 When it is finished, pin it up so that you can both admire her handiwork.

Blowing the perfect bubble

Children everywhere love blowing bubbles, and blowing the perfect bubble just needs the right bubble mix that you can supply them with. For the biggest, longest lasting bubbles, you need to add a magic ingredient to your detergent-and-water mix. Then, with a few clever twists of wire, you can make fantastic bubble wands and you're set for hours of fun with your children.

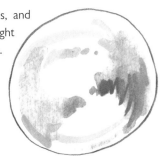

You will need
- 2400 ml (4 1/4 pints) of water
- 960 ml (32 fl oz) washing-up liquid
- 240 ml (8 fl oz) of glucose syrup
- A plastic-coated wire clothes hanger
- Floral netting or plastic-coated chicken wire
- Wire-cutters
- Narrow-nose pliers

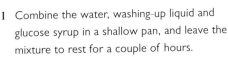

1 Combine the water, washing-up liquid and glucose syrup in a shallow pan, and leave the mixture to rest for a couple of hours.

2 While the mixture is resting, you can start making the bubble wand. Start by taking a coat hanger. Holding it by the hook, pull the opposite end down to open out the loop.

3 Using the wire-cutters, cut off the hook and the neck of the hanger, then straighten out the remaining wire to give you a straight length.

4 Using narrow-nose pliers, twist a small hook at one end of the wire. Make it about as big as the wire is around – you'll see why in just a minute.

5 Bend that end around, and hook it on to the wire about 23 cm (9 in) from the opposite end. This should give you a circle at the end of the wand about 18 cm (7 in) in diameter.

6 Squeeze the hook around the wire with pliers to keep the circle held in place, and straighten the long end of the wire. At the bottom, bunch the last few inches together to form a handle, so your children can get a good grip on it when the time comes to start making bubbles.

7 Cut a circle of floral netting or chicken wire about 20 cm (8 in) in diameter. With pliers, fold the edge of the netting tightly around the frame, snipping off any sharp ends. You should now have a long bubble wand with a loop at the end that has wire mesh across it.

8 Now you can start blowing bubbles. Take the bubble mixture and the wand to an open space, preferably outside, as you don't want spilt mixture staining your furnishings. Then your children just have to dip the wands in the mixture and wave the wands around or blow through them to make great bubbles.

9 Their instinct might be to blow as hard as they can to get the biggest bubbles, but in fact blowing gently but steadily is the best way to make them grow. Younger children might need a bit of help at first.

Making fancy dress costumes

It is handy to have a few simple costume ideas that you can fall back on at any time of the year for parties or just for when the need arises. When choosing a fancy dress costume for your child, there are a few things to bear in mind. Furry animal costumes, for example, are extremely hot and uncomfortable for any length of time. Similarly, it is inadvisable to dress young children in masks for long periods due to the danger of suffocation.

A princess/angel costume

This is a straightforward costume which, with one or two minor additions, will work for a princess or an angel. Start with a long dress. The dress is easily made with an old nightdress or a bridesmaid's dress. Obviously if you are creating an angel outfit, you will want a white dress, but a princess costume works in any colour.

You will need

- A dress, such as an old nightie or bridesmaid's dress
- Lengths of trimming, such as lace, fur, feathers etc.
- A belt or a sash made of ribbon or cord
- Card, gold paint and plastic gems (for a princess)
- Wire coat hangers, silver tinsel, tights and cotton wool (for an angel)

1 Put the dress on your child and cut the length and sleeves to the right size.
2 You might need to pin the bodice to fit, but often a sash tied around her waist will be sufficient to bring the dress together.

3 Trim the neckline, cuffs and hem with lengths of trimming.

4 For the princess – fashion a tiara or crown out of card painted gold and stuck with plastic gems.

5 For the angel – use wire coat hangers to fashion the shape of a pair of wings. Stretch over an old pair of tights and glue on white cotton wool. A halo is easily made out of silver tinsel.

A pirate costume

All little boys would love to be a pirate for a day and this is a fairly easy costume to pull together.

You will need

→ A bandana
→ An old white t-shirt
→ A waistcoat
→ White fabric
→ A sash

→ A pair of navy or black sweatpants
→ Black wellington boots
→ Card
→ Silver foil

1 Cut the sleeves of the white t-shirt to make it look a bit tattered.

2 Cut a skull and crossbones out of the white fabric and glue or stitch these on to the back of the waistcoat.

3 Tuck his sweatpants into his wellingtons.

4 Tie the bandana around your child's head and a sash around his middle.

5 Cut out a cutlass from card and cover it in silver foil.

Fly a kite

On a bright gusty day, it's a shame to keep your child cooped up indoors – you should take every opportunity to take her out for a bit of fresh air and fun in the great outdoors. But, instead of just going for a walk, why not take a kite and have some fun?

1 The most important thing about flying a kite is to make sure you do it in an open area, away from trees and power lines. Depending on the age of your child, she might be able launch the kite for herself, or you may need to do it for her.

2 Let out a small length of kite string and, holding the string in your hand, run with the kite behind you into the wind until the kite lifts it. Then let out the string until the kite reaches a good height.

3 If you have launched the kite for your child, this is the time to hand it over. Do so carefully, without tugging the string too much, to make sure the kite doesn't drop. If the wind drops, she can run into the wind or pull on the string to give the kite some extra lift.

4 Bring the kite down by slowly winding the kite string around the kite spool, and catch it just before it hits the ground to avoid damaging it.

Always stay away from electrical lines. If the kite becomes entangled, leave it there. Never fly a kite during bad weather such as a thunderstorm, as a kite can act like a lightning conductor, or in very windy weather, as young children may find holding onto the kite too difficult. Check the weather forecast first.

Games to play in the car

It is quite useful to have a variety of games to keep kids amused on long car journeys, particularly when they start the constant questioning of 'Are we nearly there yet?'

My Father Owns a Shop

There are a lot of variations of this game. Start by deciding all together what type of shop you will have – for instance, a greengrocers. The first version is a guessing game:

1   The first player says 'My father owns a greengrocers and in it he has something beginning with the letter A'. Then everyone has to guess what the answer is.
2   The player who gets it right takes the next turn, choosing something beginning with B, and so forth, right through the alphabet.

The second version is a memory test:

1   The first player says 'My father owns a greengrocers and in it he has some apples' (something beginning with the letter A).
2   The second player repeats the sentence and after 'apples' adds something beginning with B, like 'bananas'. And so each player has to remember the list and add an item for the next letter of the alphabet.

I Spy

This is an old favourite – fun for old and young alike.

1   The first player says 'I spy, with my little eye, something beginning with…' and says the first letter of the item he has picked out.

2   Then everyone must try and guess what it is.

3   The winner then has to choose the next item to guess.

4   It helps to clarify the rules before you begin, for example, the item has to be something you can see rather than something you have imagined, and has to be outside (or inside) the car.

Car Bingo

This takes a little bit of preparation, but before you go on your journey, you will need to print out some 'Bingo' cards – a page with perhaps ten things that you will probably see on your travels, for example, a flock of sheep, a church, a blue lorry etc.

1   Give each passenger a card and get them to cross off each picture as they see the object.

2   The first one to cross off all the pictures on their card shouts 'Bingo' to win!

The Animal Game

1   Each passenger must keep a look out for farm animals, like dogs, pigs, cows, sheep and so forth.

2   As soon as he spots an animal, he must make the noise of that animal to claim a point.

3   As a family, decide in advance how many points are allotted to each animal. Perhaps less common farm animals, like llamas or ostriches (depending on where exactly you are driving!) might get five points, whereas a cow or a sheep might only get one point.

4   The winner is the first one to get ten points.

Beach and lakeside outings

The secret of a successful waterside outing is all in the preparation. You will need to pack for a change in the weather and take equipment and toys to keep the children amused, as well as any necessary safety items such as rubber rings or water wings. You will need something to sit on and something to keep off the sun or the wind.

This might seem like a lot of kit, and you probably don't need all of it unless you are going to spend the whole day on the water. However, it is always better to be well-prepared. The weather can change quite suddenly, so having warm clothes to throw on when the sun goes behind a cloud is a good idea, as areas on the water can be chilly places once the sun has gone. Take a big t-shirt or cover up to put on the kids when they have had enough sun, and something they can easily wear in the water if they are going for a swim.

Family fun and games

When you have young children on a beach trip, you can forget lying back, relaxing and getting a tan. You not only need to keep an eye on them in case they decide to run into the water on their own, but they may run out of their own entertainments.

There are plenty of things you can pack to help keep them entertained. Try inflatables to use in the water, a football, frisbee, swingball or cricket set. If you're going to the beach, buckets and spades are a great idea, while if you're heading to a lake or river you could throw in fishing nets and jam jars – trying to catch tadpoles or little fish will keep them entertained for hours.

Ideas for games

Treasure hunt	Give the kids a list of things to collect, like five different pebbles, five different shells, three different types of seaweed, a piece of driftwood, etc.
Ball games	These are perfect for outdoors as you can play a variety of different games with minimal equipment so that children don't get bored. Try volleyball, cricket, swing ball, football, rounders, baseball, or just plain 'catch' in the water.
Hopscotch	Draw a grid in the sand and play with pebbles.
Frisbee	A perfect game for playing on the sand or in the water.
Sandcastles	Have a sandcastle-building competition. Who can make the biggest, or the most imaginative castle?
Rockpooling	See who can find the most unusual item or the most interesting shells.
Inflatables	These can be fun in the water, although you will need to keep a close eye on the kids. They are not an alternative to proper safety equipment like life jackets and water wings.
Flying a kite	If the wind is moderately strong and in the right direction, kite flying is a beach-friendly pastime.

Have a picnic

Whether you're attending an outdoor concert, having a day at the beach or lake, or simply heading to your local park or into your own back garden, eating outdoors is always a treat for your family, and a fun activity to do together. To make sure it all goes without a hitch, and you have a day of only good memories, there are a few things you will need to think about beforehand.

Planning ahead

The one thing that can really ruin a picnic is bad weather, so make sure you take a few precautions. If it's hot, make sure your food is suitably chilled, and remember the sunscreen. If it's cloudy, a large umbrella can save the day. You also want to make it comfortable for everyone, so pack a picnic rug or some lightweight camping chairs.

To keep everyone entertained, pack a ball, fishing rod or frisbee. You could even take some cord and rig up a makeshift volleyball net or limbo.

Plan ahead the food you want to bring. Think about scale: is it going to be a simple snack in the park or a fresh-air feast? If you have a group of families going, why not suggest that each family brings a favourite dish to share? Also bear in mind other people's food preferences, for example vegetarians or any food allergies that people may have.

Food ideas

Sandwiches	The obvious choice of food for a picnic is sandwiches. Make a good variety to cater to all tastes, vegetarians included. If you want to vary the theme, you could also try a selection of tortilla wraps, mini pittas or bagels, all with a favourite filling.
Salads	These don't have to be of the green variety. Include pasta, potato or rice salads as well. Make sure you pack them in a sealed tub.
Finger food	Include small finger foods to snack on, such as pizza slices or sausage rolls.
Vegetables	Cherry tomatoes, cucumber chunks, and carrot, celery or red and green pepper sticks work well.
Fruits	Depending on what is in season, try grapes, strawberries, cherries, or any favourite fresh fruit, kiwi fruit, dried apricots, mixed fruits, raisins, pineapple or ring pull cans of fruit in juice.
Desserts	Sweet treats are an important part of a picnic feast. Try cupcakes or a delicious homemade pie (see pages 34 and 36 for recipes).

Lemonade

Homemade lemonade is a wonderful way to cool down on a hot summer's day. This is a tried and tested favourite for children, and easy to make for large gatherings if you're going on a picnic or for a day at the beach. The flavour of freshly-squeezed lemon juice wins hands down over any store-bought variety.

How to make lemonade

You will need
+ 250 ml (8 fl oz) of freshly squeezed lemon juice (about 4–6 lemons)
+ 1 litre (1 3/4 pints) of cold water
+ 250 ml (8 fl oz) of hot water
+ 125–250 ml (4–8 fl oz) of sugar (according to taste)
+ A small saucepan

1 Dissolve the sugar in the hot water by heating it in the saucepan over a low heat until fully dissolved (this mixture is known as sugar syrup).
2 Add the lemon juice and the sugar syrup to a jug.
3 Add the cold water, until it reaches the desired strength.
4 Put in the refrigerator for 30 to 40 minutes.
5 Serve with ice and a slice of lemon. Perfect!

Treasure hunts

Treasure hunts are excellent fun for all the family, whatever your age. They can be long, complicated affairs involving dressing-up and solving clues, or just a simple search for sweets round the garden. There are different types of treasure hunts but the basic idea is the same – players must search for 'treasure'. This is a traditional activity at Easter time, when parents often hide chocolate eggs around the garden for their children to find, but it makes a great game at any time of the year, particularly for children's parties.

Simple Easter egg hunt

The simplest way to throw a treasure hunt is to hide chocolate eggs or sweets around the garden before the guests arrive. Allow about ten per child and don't make it too tricky. You'd be surprised how difficult it is, for young children especially, to see the plainly obvious! Hide them on top of flower pots, nestled in the grass or on the lowest branches of trees. Just remember not to hide anything above their shoulder height because they just won't see it. Each child gets to eat the bounty he has found, but the one with the most also gets a prize – if you are doing this at Easter, perhaps a giant egg.

Scavenger hunt

Another variation is to give each child, or each team of children, the same list of items to collect and they must go out looking for them. This can be done outside or inside and doesn't have to be particularly clever. Small children will be quite content searching for a shell, a leaf, a twig or a flower, but you can make it more sophisticated for older children. For instance, the list might include 'something that is green' or 'something that is furry'. Of course, the winners are the first team to bring back everything on the list.

Treasure hunt with clues

A treasure hunt with clues is a popular activity for older children. Divide them up into teams and start by giving them their first clue. The idea is that each team must figure out the answer to the clue, which should then lead them to another destination where they must hunt for the next clue, and so on until they have solved all the clues and discovered the whereabouts of the hidden 'treasure'.

Have fun writing the clues – use riddles or a secret code to provide an extra challenge for older children. For a party, you might like to give the game a theme – for example, a Pirate Treasure Hunt. Ask all your guests to come to the party in fancy dress as pirates. Perhaps you could draw a map of the garden showing certain 'landmarks' which you can refer to in your clues. Of course, if the garden isn't big enough, with a little bit of forward planning you could hold your treasure hunt in the local park.

Treasure hunts can also be fun for young children, as long as you make sure it is appropriate for their age group: don't make it too long or complicated as they'll lose interest. If the game is taking place away from your home, make sure everyone stays together and within your sight.

Birthday party

Everyone wants to throw the best birthday party for their child that will be the envy of other mothers (the children themselves don't mind so much as long as there is cake). However, kid's parties can be a nightmare unless you are extremely organised. Dealing with more than a handful of over-excited, sugar-high children can drive even the most patient mother to distraction. Here are a few tips which will make the party go a little more smoothly.

Party planning

Firstly, decide how many kids you want to invite. You don't have to invite every child in the class, a small handful of five or six is a perfect number for a toddler's tea party. If you do want to go all out and invite every child in the class, have your party in the garden and get extra help in the form of willing parents. If any mother offers to stay, accept gratefully, and put her to work immediately before she can change her mind.

Involve your child as much as possible. Let them help decide on the guest list, perhaps choose a theme, design invitations and help decorate. It can be fun to have a fancy dress party, but make it optional. Not all kids are natural show offs (and remember who it is who has to make the costume).

Two hours is really quite long enough for a young children's party. Any longer and the children are in danger of getting bored or over-excited – and this usually results in bad behaviour! Decide on a date, and check it doesn't coincide with another big event or holiday. It is better to throw your party in term time when you know your child's classmates are more likely to be around. Make sure you clearly state on the invitations the time, the place and the date – you might want to add directions if your house is hard to find. Send them out at least a fortnight in advance.

Party planning checklist

+ Choose date, time and a theme, if you are having one.
+ Write your guest list.
+ Send out invitations and make sure people RSVP so that you know how many guests you are expecting on the day.
+ Decide what food you will serve, and whether you will buy a birthday cake or make one yourself.
+ Plan games and gather together or make any necessary props.
+ Select appropriate music, both to have on in the background and to use for any party games.
+ Buy decorations (streamers, balloons, party poppers and birthday banners), appropriate prizes for games, wrapping paper and food.
+ Prepare the birthday tea. If you're making a cake, decide if you are going to be creative with a shape or theme for the cake.
+ Blow up the balloons and decorate your party area well in advance. You don't want to still be getting things ready when the first guests arrive.
+ Have a great party!

Make a birthday cake

The best way to produce a delicious birthday cake which your child will love is to start by making a plain Victoria Sponge. You can't go wrong with a proper old-fashioned sponge cake and the advantage is that you can go to town with the decorating and dress it up to suit the occasion. It is so easy to do – all you need is equal quantities of butter, sugar and flour, and some eggs.

To make a small Victoria Sponge cake you will need

- → 2 loose-bottomed 18 cm (7 in) cake tins
- → 110g (3 3/4 oz) butter or margarine
- → 110g (3 3/4 oz) caster sugar
- → 2 medium eggs
- → 110g (3 3/4oz) self raising flour

1 Heat the oven to 180°C/350°F.
2 Grease two loose-bottomed 18 cm (7 in) cake tins with a little butter or line with baking parchment.
3 Beat the butter and the sugar together until pale and creamy.
4 Gradually beat in the eggs, adding a little at a time.
5 Sieve the flour into the mixture and use a large metal spoon to fold in gently.
6 Divide the mixture between the cake tins and smooth the surface of each.
7 Bake for 20–25 minutes or until a skewer comes out clean.
8 Cool on a wire rack.

Decorating themes

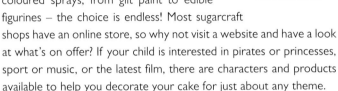

There are all sorts of products available from professional cake decorating suppliers that can really give your cake an individual special look. From sugar flowers to coloured sprays, from gilt paint to edible figurines – the choice is endless! Most sugarcraft shops have an online store, so why not visit a website and have a look at what's on offer? If your child is interested in pirates or princesses, sport or music, or the latest film, there are characters and products available to help you decorate your cake for just about any theme.

Icing options

You may prefer to keep it simple and just sandwich the cake together with jam, with a sprinkling of icing sugar sifted over the top, or you might like to make your own frosting. Try using orange or lemon juice instead of water to mix icing sugar into a paste with a citrus zing. Butter icings are also popular and can be coloured with a drop of edible colouring. Beat a quantity of butter until soft and creamy, and then mix together with twice the amount of icing sugar.

Shapes and moulds

If you are feeling more adventurous, try a mould and bake the cake in a fun shape. You can use a bowl or any ovenproof container to create an unusual shape, so get creative. You can also bake two cakes and use one to cut out sponge shapes to 'glue' on to the other with icing. To improvise a piping bag cut out of a large corner of a plastic bag. Fill it with icing, snip a tiny bit off the end and write your message!

Party food

The secret of successful catering for a children's party is all about size. Children seem to love miniature food, and little dishes piled high with a colourful abundance of bite-size goodies makes for a really enticing party table, and it doesn't have to cost a fortune. Try chicken and mango kebabs, sweet potato wedges, homemade mini burgers, muffin pizzas, interestingly shaped sandwiches, and of course, jelly and ice-cream, with the all-important birthday cake as the main attraction. Remember that this isn't the time to be too fussy about sugar and additives – it is a special occasion, after all.

Keep it simple

You are going to have quite a lot on your hands without over-complicating the food, so try and keep it simple. It wouldn't be cheating, for example, to buy most of it ready made from the stores, so that all you have to do is get it into the oven. That will remove some of the stress of preparation, and leave you free to concentrate all your culinary skills on the birthday cake.

Homemade treats

If you do want to show off your culinary prowess, try your hand at making a birthday treat like a jelly. Of course anyone can make a jelly using a packet, but for a special occasion like a child's birthday party it can be much more satisfying and definitely more eye-catching to make a jelly from scratch – you can vary this recipe according to what fruits are in season.

How to make grape jelly

You will need
→ 500 ml (17 fl oz) red grape juice
→ 4 teaspoons powdered gelatine
→ Some red grapes
→ Party bowls

1 Put six tablespoons of grape juice into a small saucepan and slowly sprinkle the gelatine powder over it. Set aside for between 5–10 minutes.
2 Return the saucepan to a low heat and allow the gelatine to melt slowly – do not let it boil.
3 Gradually stir in the remaining grape juice, making sure that it is well blended.
4 Wash, halve and, if necessary, de-seed the grapes. Arrange the grapes in the bottom of individual party bowls.
5 Carefully pour the jelly mixture over the grapes. Place the bowls in the fridge until just starting to set. Top with more grape halves, then return to the fridge to set completely.

Of course, there's nothing stopping you from making a range of treats – you could try cupcakes (see page 36) or, for something really special, homemade lemonade (see page 102).

Party games

For any children's party you need to have some party games in mind to keep them entertained. There are many children's games to choose from – you'll probably remember how to play them from your own childhood. When choosing your games, bear in mind how many children you will have at the party, how messy or noisy the game is, and how much preparation or equipment is needed to set it up. The general rule, for your own peace of mind, is to keep it simple. Otherwise you'll spend hours setting it all up and tidying up afterwards. Don't forget that for many games you'll need some jolly music. Depending on their age, try a compilation of nursery rhymes, or TV tunes or even some light pop music.

Don't feel that you need to have activities organised for every single moment of the party. Small children are quite happy playing with toys, particularly other people's, so get a box of your kid's stuff ready in advance and that will keep them happy for at least half an hour. When you do have organised games, remember to keep them simple and not too competitive.

Prizes and treats

You can't have enough prizes – young children can be surprisingly competitive. Buy giant size bags of chocolates and sweets and hand them out at will. You could also have some slightly more substantial prizes, for the final stage of pass the parcel for example, although these don't need to be expensive; something small like a set of colouring pens or a set of stickers should be fine. The thrill of having won the prize will probably be enough to satisfy most children.

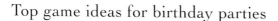

Top game ideas for birthday parties

Musical chairs	When the music stops the players must find a chair. The player without a chair is out. For variations on this theme, try musical bumps (all players sit on the floor when the music stops) or musical statues (everyone stands still when the music stops).
Pin the tail on the donkey	Each player must try to pin the tail in the correct place while blindfolded. Whoever is closest to the correct place wins.
Sleeping lions	Get everyone to lie down, keep very still and pretend to be asleep. Then you must try and 'wake' them by saying funny things or tickling them. If they move, they're out.
Blind man's buff	Put a blindfold on one player, and twizzle her around several times in the middle of the room. She must then guess the name of the next player she can find, just by feeling their face. If she gets it right, she can pass them the blindfold and it is their turn to be the blind man.
Pass the parcel	Wrap small treats like sweets into the layers, as well as the main prize in the middle. When the music stops the person holding the parcel can unwrap a layer.

Advanced Mum

→ Surviving your child's first date

→ Getting dressed in five minutes

→ Pampering yourself

→ Planning a romantic getaway

→ Getting breakfast in bed

Do you know how to make a Margarita? Do you want breakfast in bed? Well, you're about to find out how, along with many other ways to become an Advanced Mum. Learn from ideas designed for Mum to help her find more time for herself and Dad, planning a girls' night out with her friends, and even more tricky dilemmas like dealing with a teenage party or applying your make-up on the run. These top tips for Advanced Mums will transform you into Super-Mum!

Your child's appearance

Whatever your child wears, however he chooses to dress, anything you say on the subject is liable to either antagonise or offend him, so it's best to bite your tongue! As much as his experimentations make you shudder, try not to comment. As your child grows up he will naturally be looking for ways to explore his individuality and the way he dresses is an obvious sign of this. Even innocent comments from you that weren't really meant as criticism, can dent his self-confidence – and he most likely won't listen to your opinion anyway. So instead, here are a few things to consider which may help you turn a blind eye . . .

Changing phases

However bad this week's outfit is, remember that it can always get worse! Most likely it's a passing phase and really not worth jumping up and down about it. Remember what you were like and which of your fashion choices drove your mother mad. She despaired of your hippy flares as much as you despair of his gothic black. Worry about his school work instead – that will have a far more profound effect on the rest of his life than his current haircut.

Don't overreact

Your kids desperately want a reaction from you – after all, what young person really wants their parents' approval of their latest outfit? Quite often he may just be trying to wind you up, so don't respond and with any luck the offending garment won't reappear.

Rules and compromise

Try and agree on some ground rules. If it is just a matter of your differing tastes, don't push it. Let it go. There are far more important things to be worried about, for instance – anything that is permanent like piercings or tattoos, or clothing that offends in anyway or is provocative (beware of giving children ideas they hadn't thought of in these discussions, otherwise it's going to prove counter-productive). These are the issues you should be saving your consternation for. Together you need to decide where the boundaries are and if something is likely to give genuine offence to another person, whether this is religious, cultural or sexual.

At the end of the day, if your child has good manners, a kind heart and a great attitude, leave him be! This is the only time in his life when he will really have the freedom to express himself before adult life demands he adheres to certain conventions.

Survive your child's first date

Your child's first date will be a milestone event in their lives, but one that can cause great anxiety for parents. There is so much at stake, or so it feels. It is inevitable that you will spend the whole evening on tenterhooks but with some preparation you might be able to allay the worst of your fears.

Meeting your child's date

Invite your child's date home first so that you can meet her. It might help to put any fears you have to rest if you can put a face to the name, and she may turn out to be a perfectly wonderful human being that you'd be delighted to welcome into your family. Of course, you may end up wishing she had never darkened your doorstep, but in much the same way that it does not pay to criticise your child's choice of dress, neither does it achieve anything to criticise his choice of date. Don't waste time being judgmental – like his outfits, his dates may also change from week to week.

Try to keep embarrassing or negative comments to a minimum. Reaching for the photo albums of babies in baths may well be tempting but will not be a popular move with your teenager. Recounting embarrassing stories from his youth, bad jokes and family video footage also fall into this category.

Be available to talk to your teenager about the date when he returns if there is anything he wants to discuss with you. Of course, he may have no desire whatsoever to discuss it, in which case don't push the point or he may feel as if you're prying.

Setting some ground rules

It is a good idea to lay down some ground rules for dating to give yourself at least a little peace of mind while they're out.

- Agree a time by which he needs to be in. Don't be swayed by pleading for a later curfew — you don't want to be up until midnight worrying about him getting in safely. Set an earlier curfew if he is going out on a weeknight.
- Completely forbid drinking and driving, and make it clear that this ban applies to him getting into a car with anyone else who has been drinking and intends to drive.
- Make sure he has a mobile telephone with him, or enough change to use a public telephone. He must ring you if there is any reason at all that they might be late (while reminding him that being late is against the rules!).

Even after you have laid down the ground rules, it basically boils down to trust. You must let go and trust your child. Trust that you have brought him up properly. Trust that he will do the right thing and behave in the right way. Unless you are going to accompany your children and chaperone them on all their dates (which will be about as unpleasant for you as it will be for them!), there is nothing else you can do but trust them unless they give you reason not to.

Gatecrash your teenager's party

Sooner or later your teenager is going to ask you if he can have a party. This request does not need to strike fear into your heart. It is possible to throw a teenager's party with your teen and a) remain on speaking terms and b) end up with an event that both you and he will feel comfortable with. He may see it as gatecrashing, but if you are fond of your house the way it is, it's best to not stray too far from home during at least the first few parties he throws, until he's shown you that you can expect your home to remain intact. Planning out the details with him is the best way to make sure it all goes smoothly.

Planning the party

1 Sit down with your teenager and discuss every aspect of the party. Decide on the important things first like the date, budget, number of guests, the venue, a theme, entertainment, music and the menu.

2 Draw up a list of tasks that need to be done and decide who will be responsible for sorting out each job. It's not your event so don't get stuck doing all the work. If he wants to throw a party, he has to put in the effort.

3 At this point, it is sensible to set down some ground rules. Let him contribute to this process so that the rules are a joint effort between you both. Discuss things like where party-goers are allowed to go and where is out of bounds (this would be a good time to unearth a key to your bedroom door). Decide how you will deal with any uninvited guests who turn up.

4 Agree an end time. Inform your neighbours in advance that there will be a party but that the music will be turned off at a reasonable time.

5   Discuss the subject of alcohol. This can be a sticky subject as for most young people a party is not really a party unless there is the promise of a beer or two. You will need to consider the age of your child and his friends, and the laws about providing alcohol to children, and take steps to ensure your partygoers stick to the rules (maybe lock the liquor cabinet and throw away the key!).

6   Food will also need to be provided and it is best to play safe and go for simple fare like pizza slices, chicken wings, burgers and chips. Plastic plates and glasses are marvellously easy to clear up – there is no washing up required, just tip them all into the recycling bin.

7   If you are intending to remain at the party to keep an eye on the proceedings, why not ask some of the other parents to join you for your own party in another room? If this idea really doesn't go down well with your teenager, or if you simply can't bear to stick around with that many noisy teenagers invading your house, agree that you will stay out of the way but within calling distance.

8   It is not a bad idea to make your presence felt from time to time during the evening, just so that the guests know there is an adult in the house.

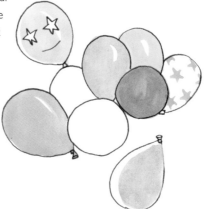

Romance Dad

In the daily grind of work, household chores and caring for the children, it is easy to lose sight of the romance in your relationship with your husband. After a few years of marriage, those romantic moments which made your first months together really special, can seem like a lifetime away. However, with just a little bit of effort you can make time for each other and keep the romance alive! It is all about reconnecting and strengthening the ties between you that make you both interested in each other as people, not just as Mum and Dad.

Spending time together

Talk every day. Make time to communicate. Tell each other how your day went, what your worries are, what your triumphs have been. Keep talking and you will stay the best of friends, even if there are moments when the romance dims slightly.

Try and do something nice for each other regularly. Give him a treat, a reason to feel good about himself. Run him a bath when he gets home from work and take him a glass of wine. Make his favourite dessert. Book him a game of golf. Show him that you think about his needs and want him to feel valued. And of course make sure he returns the favour.

One way to strengthen the ties between you is to indulge in some shared interests. Take up a hobby that you can do together and appeals to you both. Don't try and do everything together, you'll end up driving each other crazy. But the occasional shared activity will give you both an area of common interest and something to talk about apart from the children. At the very least, go for a walk together.

Dating

The bet is that you have stopped flirting with each other. It is difficult to feel flirty when you are up to your elbows in dirty nappies or dirty dishes, but you shouldn't give up on it. Hire a babysitter once a week and have a regular date night. Go out together and enjoy being alone with each other. Take the time to get dressed up, kiss in the back row of the cinema, play footsie under the restaurant table, and hold hands as you walk down the street. Don't talk about work or the kids – just concentrate on re-connecting with each other.

Ideas for date night

> + **Have dinner out together** (somewhere that doesn't have to be child-friendly for a change!). Be adventurous and try new restaurants and different types of cuisine.
> + **Movie night.** If you want to see the latest rom-com and he wants to see car chases, take it turns to choose a movie (and don't complain at his choices).
> + **A romantic night in.** Don't eat with the kids that night, but set the table with candles, flowers and a bottle of wine.
> + **Watch the sunset together.** Find a romantic spot, whether it's a restaurant with a beautiful view, or just a park bench if it's not too cold.
> + **Treat yourselves.** Date night doesn't always need to be an expensive night, but try and save up toward the occasional night when you can really treat yourselves, whether it's with a bottle of champagne, or booking into a luxury hotel.

Get dressed in five minutes

Getting dressed in five minutes is a trick all mothers need to learn. There is bound to be a morning, if not every morning, when you are running late and need to get ready in a flash (and the less time you spend getting ready, the longer you have to stay in bed). If you get into good habits early on, five minutes is all you need to get dressed every morning, whether you are in a tremendous hurry or not!

The thing that takes the most time is not actually putting on your clothes, it is choosing your outfit. For busy mums, knowing exactly what you are going to wear and only having to step into it is one less thing to think about. Having only five minutes in which to dress is the usual state of affairs for a lot of mums, especially those who work outside the home. Follow these tips and it need not be stressful!

Ready to wear

It is frustrating to pull out an item of clothing from your wardrobe only to find that it has an unsightly stain or is missing a button (although not as frustrating as only noticing once you have already left the house). To avoid wasting precious seconds this way, never put away any item of clothing unless it is clean and ready to wear. This also means it must not require mending – there are no rips or tears, all buttons are present and correct, and the hem is not falling down. If you stick to this rule, it means that everything you pull out of your wardrobe is good to go.

Organise your wardrobe

Keep your wardrobe sensibly organised, otherwise you will find it impossible to locate the jacket you need in a hurry. This means having a regular sort out and getting rid of clothing that you no longer wear. It also means keeping your drawers and wardrobe tidy, so that t-shirts are all stored together, trousers are all hung together, hats are in one drawer and underwear in another, and so on. Don't be tempted to just stuff things back in and close the door. You'll regret it next time you only have five minutes to get dressed! If you want to be super-organised, pack away your clothes that are out of season so that you don't have unseasonal items getting in your way.

Planning ahead

It helps to have some co-ordinated outfits that you know are tried and tested, that you have worn before and that you know work really well. For example: an occasion outfit for weddings and christenings; a business outfit for meetings and job interviews; an evening outfit for parties and dinners etc. This will help cut down on the amount of time you spend trying to decide what to wear.

Out the door

Keeping your clothes organised and ready to wear should give you a good start. Now grab your pre-planned outfit, remember your multi-tasking skills (all mothers should be able to perform such tasks as putting on socks while brushing your hair at the same time without falling over), and you really can be out the door in five minutes flat.

Speed shopping

There are many ways you can reduce the time you spend grocery shopping – the secret is to be very organised! If you plan your menus, combine ingredients, write a shopping list, shop alone or via the Internet, you can get it done in no time at all.

Plan your route

If you decide what you will cook in advance and then write a shopping list accordingly, you are less likely to wander around the shop wasting precious time trying to decide what groceries to purchase or whether you have run out of frozen peas. This also has the added bonus of saving you money because you know that you only need what is on your list. You will probably find that you don't need to buy as much as you thought! Keep hold of your list – discovering that you have left it behind on the kitchen table will not speed up your shopping excursion.

Combine ingredients

When planning your menus and writing your shopping list, try and use ingredients for more than one meal – so for instance, potatoes could be roasted with a joint of meat on Sunday and then mashed for a cottage pie with minced beef on Tuesday. The leftovers of the roast meat could make a curry on Monday with rice, which could be used again with the remaining minced beef to provide chilli con carne on Thursday, and so forth. Not only is this the most economical way to shop, it is also much quicker as you are buying a greatly reduced number of items.

Internet shopping

Buying groceries over the Internet is now a very quick and simple process. Most major supermarkets have a facility whereby you can save your most commonly purchased items into an online shopping list. This cuts down a huge amount of time, as once you have set it up you can quickly access your favourite items rather than search the whole online store for a particular product. The other major time saver is that they will deliver your groceries to your front door for a small charge, meaning that you do not even have to leave the house.

Shop alone

Another way to cut down on the time you spend grocery shopping is never to take your family with you unless you really have to! They slow you down, ask for items not on your shopping list, put things in the trolley you don't want, and generally behave in a way that can be stressful and demands your time. So don't take them with you! Schedule the shopping for when they are at school or agree with your husband that you will go to the supermarket while he entertains the troops at home. If you really must go to the shops when you have your children with you, try giving each of them one item on the list to find – it will at least keep them occupied, although it is no guarantee it will get the job done any quicker.

It is important for Mum and Dad to allow each other a bit of personal time and space occasionally. Take an evening off every now and then, whether you spend it at home on your own with a good book and a luxurious bubble bath, or out on the town with friends.

Mums' night in

A mums' night in is a great way for mothers to socialise without either great expense or the need to organise babysitters. It works best if a group of you take it in turns to host an evening, perhaps once a month, and everyone comes over to your house, leaving their children at home with their spouses. You may all feel like you don't get to go out much, especially if you have young children, so arrange an activity which feels a little bit indulgent as well as fun.

Mums' night in themes

Movie night	Gather the girls together and watch the latest chick flick!
Karaoke party	Hire in a karaoke machine and you can spend the evening warbling along to all your favourite hits.
Clothes swap	Ask all your friends to bring any clothing or accessories they no longer want and have a swapping session.
Pamper party	Invite everyone round for an evening of girly fun, giving each other facials, manicures and pedicures, experimenting with new hairstyles, testing out new beauty products and exchanging beauty tips.
Book exchange	If you don't have the time to commit to a regular book club, get all your girlfriends to bring along a book they have recently enjoyed. Take it in turns to tell each other a little bit about your book and finish by exchanging with someone else who would like to read it.

Making cocktails

Knowing how to put together a few classic cocktails is useful for entertaining, even if it's just for a night in with the girls.

Kit and ingredients

To make good cocktails you will need a choice of spirits and fruit juices, some ice, fresh fruit for garnishes and a cocktail shaker and glasses. You can serve cocktails in just about any glass of course, but as a rule of thumb, stemmed cocktail glasses are usually used for drinks served without ice, and tumblers for those on the rocks.

The quality of your ingredients will determine whether you make an average or an excellent cocktail. Cheap, low quality spirits taste most unpleasant when mixed in a cocktail and will really affect the taste. Similarly, fruit juice can elevate a cocktail to perfection if it is freshly squeezed.

Sugar syrup is a common cocktail ingredient. You can buy it from specialist shops but it is easy to make yourself at home. Put equal quantities of water and sugar in a saucepan and heat until the sugar has dissolved. Boil for a minute without stirring and leave to cool.

Margarita

You will need
→ I part triple-sec
→ 2 parts lime juice
→ 3 parts tequila

Combine ingredients in cocktail shaker and serve in a glass – the rim dipped in lemon or lime juice and then in salt.

Classic Martini

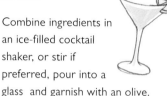

You will need
→ 1 part dry vermouth
→ 2 parts gin
→ dash Angostura bitters

Combine ingredients in an ice-filled cocktail shaker, or stir if preferred, pour into a glass and garnish with an olive.

Cosmopolitan

You will need
→ 3 parts vodka
→ 1 part Cointreau or triple sec
→ 1-2 parts cranberry juice
→ a splash of fresh lime juice or lime cordial

Combine ingredients in an ice-filled cocktail shaker, strain into a glass and garnish with a twist of lime.

Rum punch

You will need
→ 1 part lime or lemon juice
→ 2 part sugar syrup
→ 3 parts rum
→ 4 parts water and ice

Combine ingredients in a glass and stir well. Garnish with some grated nutmeg.

Apply make-up on the run

There are never enough hours in the day, so perfecting a swift make-up routine can really save you time and means that you won't have to worry about how you look on the school run! This is not the full war paint, just the bare essentials for those days when you really have only got five minutes.

You would be surprised just how little make-up you really need and how fresh and natural you will look. Why not keep an emergency make-up bag with spare products in the car? That way, you can leave the house in a hurry and finish your mascara at the traffic lights. Please remember that, of course, it wouldn't be safe to apply make-up while you are driving.

For a more sophisticated evening look in a hurry, try applying black eyeliner on your upper eyelid as close to the lashline as possible and then blend it with your finger or a tissue to create a smoky-eyed look. Try using a coloured lip pencil before your gloss to define your lip outline and then colour your lips in.

Just the basics

- ❖ Apply a little powder foundation to any areas that require extra coverage.
- ❖ Use a skin highlighter on under-eye shadows if necessary.
- ❖ Swipe light colour eyeshadow over eyelids.
- ❖ Apply mascara.
- ❖ Swipe lip balm or neutral gloss over lips.

Look for products that do more than one thing – for instance, powder that acts as foundation; concealer and powder all in one; or use an eyeshadow as eyeliner. This will save you plenty of time and you'll have fewer products to keep in your emergency make-up bag.

Mums' night out

Getting together with your other mum friends for a night out is a great way to let off some steam. Spoil yourself for an evening, have a well-deserved night off from the children and a good laugh with your girlfriends. It is a perfect opportunity to let your hair down and pour your heart out – and being a mum means you don't get to do either very often!

Babysitting

Of course, it should be easy to organise babysitting for a mum's night out, as the dads will be able to stay home! Get in some beers and his favourite take-away and promise that you will watch the kids when he wants to have a dad's night out!

Who to invite

When planning your night out, you will need to decide who you are going to ask and what you are all going to do. Make sure that everyone in the group gets along and, tempting though it might be to include your other friends, keep your invitations to mothers only. This way you have all immediately got something in common and will be able to share your feelings and frustrations, as well as the funny side of motherhood, with women that really know and understand how you feel!

Sophistication and glamour

A nice way to start the evening is to ask your friends to meet at your house first. Why not greet the other mums with a sophisticated cocktail and play some of your favourite tunes? Take a few moments to unwind together and to catch up on each other's news. For an extra touch of glamour, consider hiring a limousine to chauffeur you around for the evening. It really isn't that expensive if you all chip in together and it is such fun to travel in style!

The main attraction

Liven up the evening with themes and things to do. An evening out does not have to mean an evening spent drinking, especially as most mothers will have to be up early in the morning to see to their children. That is not to say that a few drinks can't be part of the evening's entertainment, but it is a good idea to plan something else as the main attraction. Themed evenings are also fun, and this helps to make the decision of where to go and what to do.

- Take it in turns to choose a restaurant each time you go out with the girls, so that you try something different each time.
- Book an indulgent evening at a spa or beauty salon. Enjoy a massage or a facial and a few glasses of champagne.
- Go bowling together and have a few beers.
- Sign up for salsa classes or belly dancing at your local dance studio.
- Try a themed evening, for example, a Spanish evening might start with sangria, followed by a meal at a paella restaurant and then flamenco lessons. A French evening might involve dinner at a bistro and an art film with subtitles.

Get some rest

Finding a bit of time to take a break and put your feet up is essential. A mother earns her right to the occasional break, to rest a while comfortably, recharge her batteries or switch off completely after a stressful day.

Timing is everything

To enjoy an uninterrupted rest, the end of the day is often the best time to put your feet up. Wait until the children are in bed. Otherwise no sooner have you sat down there will be demands for food, drink, appreciation of artistic talents and searches for lost toys. Once they're all safely tucked up in bed, unplug the telephone or switch the answering machine on. Put some low music on the stereo – something gentle and soothing, rather than heavy rock. Light some candles or dim the lights. Pour a glass of wine.

Put your feet up!

One of the best ways to relax and unwind is to actually put your feet up. Arrange a footstool in front of your armchair so that you can elevate your feet comfortably or spread out on the sofa with your legs stretched out. Read a book, peruse the newspapers, or just lie back and let the day evaporate away. If you can persuade your husband to rub your feet, so much the better, but whatever happens, do not move for at least half an hour.

Pamper yourself

We all know how stressful being a busy mother can be. Taking some time to pamper yourself can really help you to relax – making you a much calmer person to be around and therefore a better mum!

The perfect pampering experience doesn't have to cost the earth. You don't have to travel to an expensive spa or health farm as you can pamper yourself very easily at home. The most effective de-stresser, which also feels luxurious and special, is a long, hot soak in the tub. Follow a few simple steps to make this the ultimate pampering experience.

Pampering top tips

- ✦ **Peace and quiet.** Make sure you will not be interrupted, so wait until the children are in bed and take the phone off the hook.
- ✦ **Smells and sounds.** Pour some relaxing essential oils or bubble bath into the water – lavender is very soothing. Put some classical music on the stereo and light some scented candles.
- ✦ **Unwind.** Make a calming camomile tea or pour a glass of champagne to sip while you luxuriate in the bath. Read a book, sing along with the music, or just lie there and daydream, but on no account allow yourself to think about stressful things. No worrying about work or the children!
- ✦ **Spoil yourself.** Wrap yourself in a fluffy towel, maybe paint your toenails or set your hair, but don't do anything strenuous or onerous after your bath. Why not curl up in bed with a magazine and drift off to sleep early?

If you don't have a facial mask on hand when you feel like a bit of pampering, turn to the larder. Fresh ingredients such as fruits and herbs nourish the skin, improve circulation and can tone and cleanse better than expensive shop-bought goodies. Try mashing a banana with a couple of teaspoons of honey and applying to your face for 10 minutes.

Facials

Having a facial at home is an easy way to keep up your beauty regime when you are busy. It is also a lovely way to pamper yourself when you are lying in the bath, but if time is short, you can apply your facepack and get on with the chores!

How to give yourself a facial

+ **Cleanse**. You need your skin to be squeaky-clean before you begin, so use a cleanser appropriate for your skin type to remove all dirt and make-up.
+ **Exfoliate**. Use a simple scrub to exfoliate your skin, paying particular attention to any areas prone to oiliness. Use the tips of your fingers to rub gently in a circular pattern.
+ **Steam**. This helps to open the pores so the mask can work more effectively. Wring out a washcloth in hot water and lay over your face for a few minutes.
+ **Mask**. Apply the facemask avoiding sensitive areas like your eyes and mouth. Leave on until dry or as per the instructions. You can also lay some thin slices of cucumber or two spent teabags over your eyes which can help reduce puffiness.
+ **Moisturise**. After washing the mask off gently, use a mild moisturiser to complete your skin care treatment.

Create some personal space

Creating a little private area, your own personal space, can be a godsend to the busy mum. This corner should be somewhere you can escape to and be alone with your thoughts, or just somewhere to unwind uninterrupted. Read a book, knit a scarf, watch your favourite TV programme – whatever helps you feel like you've had a little break. Even if you only have a small house and you cannot dedicate an entire room to yourself, you can still commandeer a room for a while. Send the kids off to entertain their father for an hour or so and let him take some responsibility for the children's antics. Forbid anyone from interrupting your 'me-time'.

Establishing your domain

- Clear the area of children, pets, husbands, and anything else that may interrupt your personal time.
- Start with a chair. Somewhere comfortable to sit is essential. A comfy old armchair can be dressed up. Just add some comfy cushions and a throw or blanket.
- A small table is useful. Add a lamp, your favourite books, a tin of biscuits and your personal stereo and you are all set for an indulgent hour or two.
- To really personalise your space, why not gather all your favourite cards and photographs and pin them to a corkboard which you can hang above your chair and table?

Learn something new

There is always room to learn something new, and being a mother shouldn't stop you developing your interests further. Organise yourself so that you can devote a spare hour a week to a new hobby or activity. Audio books are available on many topics and these are especially useful for learning a new hobby when you are short of time. Play them in the car while travelling to work or to fetch the children from school, or have them on in the background while you are exercising. Deciding what new hobby to take up is often the difficult part as there is so much to choose from!

Where to start

- → **Knitting.** It's not just for grannies, knitting can be trendy too.
- → **Photography.** From family portraits to holiday snaps to art form, there are many reasons to learn how to take a better picture.
- → **Salsa classes.** Dancing is a great way to keep fit if you're not into the gym, and great fun as well whether you go with friends or manage to convince your husband to accompany you.
- → **Amateur theatre.** If you have an unrealised dream of acting, see if your local community has a theatre group you can join.
- → **Skydiving.** Possibly a bit of an extreme activity for some, but if you are seeking some thrills, skydiving could be for you – your chance to see the world from a different angle!

Romantic getaways

When you have children, you suddenly realise that maintaining the romance in your relationship requires an awful lot of hard work! However, with some advanced planning it is possible to plan a relaxing weekend getaway that you will both enjoy.

How to plan a weekend getaway

1 Firstly, you will need to arrange childcare. Ask grandparents well in advance for possible dates when they would be able to look after your children for the weekend. Book them in early.

2 When choosing a location for your weekend getaway, bear in mind that the further you go from home, the shorter your weekend will be. Don't waste a precious moment travelling further than you have to and possibly think about negotiating with Granny so the weekend starts on Friday evening.

3 Your budget will probably be the deciding factor in where you go for the weekend. Don't despair if you are counting the pennies, as a romantic experience does not necessarily have to mean a costly hotel and expensive dinners. Somewhere you can spend time together alone is the only real requirement.

4 You should make an effort not to talk about either work or the children. This is a time for you both so enjoy it and don't worry about what is happening back home. Turn off your phone – if there is an emergency, Granny can phone Reception.

Breakfast in bed

If you are a mother, it is perfectly reasonable to expect breakfast in bed now and again – on Mother's Day it is practically your right. However, if you have any doubts at all about whether your family know this – especially your husband, as it will probably be his job to co-ordinate the making of the breakfast – you may have to resort to hinting, and if that doesn't work, demanding.

Don't bother being subtle. Go straight in there with something like 'Honey, I know the children will want to help you make a Mother's Day breakfast in bed tomorrow morning for me. I was thinking that just coffee and some French toast would be easy for them to do.' This should have the effect of:

> ✧ reminding him it is Mother's Day
> (don't rely on his ability to remember it without prompts)
> ✧ explaining that you want breakfast in bed
> ✧ telling him what you would like to eat
> ✧ disguising your hint as helpful advice for the children.

Make sure you have all the ingredients in the kitchen in easy view and leave any appropriate recipes open on the side before you go to bed so they have no excuse. When they bring you the tray exclaim loudly with surprise at how thoughtful they have been and how delicious it looks. The secret to getting breakfast in bed again – not just on Mother's Day – is to compliment them all and make such a fuss of your clever husband and children, that they will want to do it again to please you!

Index